HOMO SAPIENS PART - XI

HUMANITY'S EIGHTY: A COLLECTION OF POETIC REFLECTIONS

MAWPHNIANG NAPOLEON

"Dear reader,

We dedicate this eleventh book of poetry collection under the 'Homo Sapiens' Series to you, our lovely and valued reader. Your vibe and dedication to reading this work is truly appreciated by all of us on the team.

From the bottom of our hearts, we express our heartfelt gratitude for you and the time you have taken to immerse yourself in our words. You are beautiful and unique in your own ways, and we hope that these poems have touched your soul in some way.

Thank you for your presence and allowing us to share our creative expressions with you. You are loved, valued, and appreciated.

With love and gratitude,

The 'Homo Sapiens' Series Team"

Contents

Contents

Contents

Contents

Foreword

Verily, thou art what thou eateth and what thou readeth

For in thy food and in thy books, doth shape thy being

In the inner depths of thy soul, doth they bring

The wisdom and the knowledge, that to thee, doth sing.

As the grains of wheat and the seeds of corn

Are ground into flour, and then made into bread,

So too is the knowledge, which thou taketh in

Transformed, to create the essence of thy mind.

And as the body is built from what it feedeth on,

So too is the soul, from what thou readeth.

Words, written by those who have come before,

Do shape the fabric of thy thoughts, for ever more.

For each page thou turneth, doth bring a new insight,

Each chapter a different perspective to thee,

And as thou delve deeper, into the book's lore,

Thou dost find the truth, of what it really means.

And thus, thou must choose, what thou wishest to eat,

For as the body is strengthened by its food,

So too is the soul, by what thou readeth.

Therefore, be careful, in what thou feedeth thy mind.

For the knowledge of the world, can be both true and false,

And if thou art not cautious, thou may be led astray.

So, seek out the wisdom, that hath been proven right,

And let it guide thy thoughts, both day and night.

And in thy quest for truth, do not be afraid,

To embrace the knowledge, that is still unknown.

For it is in the unknown, that thou shall find,

The greatest discoveries, that shall forever bind.

So, eat of the good, and read of the wise,

For in this way, thou shall grow, both in mind and size.

For thou art what thou eateth, and what thou readeth,

And thus, shall thy spirit, be forever wreathed.

And as thou continue, in thy journey through life,

Never forget, what thou art truly made of.

For thou art the sum, of all that thou hast seen,

And all that thou hast learned, in thy quest for truth within.

And as thou grow, in wisdom and in grace,

Let thy knowledge, be a beacon to all who seek.

For in thy books and in thy food, doth lie the key,

To the secrets of the universe, for all to see.

And though the journey, may be long and hard,

Let not thy spirit, ever falter or be scarred.

For in the end, thou shall stand tall and proud,

And bask in the light, of thy knowledge-endowed.

So, eat well, and read on, with courage in thy heart,

And never forget, what thou art truly made of.

For thou art the essence, of all that is good and right,

And in this way, shall thou find, thy greatest height.

So, let thy knowledge, be a guiding light,

To all who seek the truth, in the world so bright.

And let thy books and thy food, be the keys,

To unlocking the secrets, of the universe and thee.

For thou art what thou eateth and what thou readeth,

And in this truth, shall thou find, thy greatest strength.

And so, may thy journey, be filled with wisdom and grace,

And may thou find, thy greatest truth, in this world of space. Oh Homo Sapiens, Part XI, a tome so grand,

A collection of eighty reflections divine,

A journey through humanity, oh so planned,

An exploration of our hearts and mind.

From fate to mid-life crisis, nature's guise,

Solace, self-discovery, all within,

A treatise on the human soul's bright eyes,

The wisdom of our species, found within.

The author, Mawphniang Napoleon, so wise,

A guide through life's mysteries and strife,

A master of the written word, whose prize,

Is to reveal the depths of human life.

So do not hesitate, dear reader, pick,

This book, and embark on a journey rich.

And as you delve into each verse and rhyme,

Let the words of the author be your guide.

For in his thoughts and insights, you will find,

A path to truth, to love, to self inside.

So let the words flow like a gentle stream,

And carry you away to lands untold.

Let the pages of this book be your dream,

And open doors to wisdom, yet untold.

And when your journey's end is finally near,

You'll find that you have gained a better view,

Of life's complexities, of hope and fear,

And a deeper understanding of you.

So let this book be a companion true,

On your journey through life, and through its due.

With love and gratitude,

The 'Homo Sapiens' Series Team"

Preface

"The essence of being human is a never-ending journey of self-discovery and reflection. In this eleventh installment of the Homo Sapiens series, Mawphniang Napoleon takes us on a poetic journey through the complexities of the human experience. Through his carefully crafted verses, we are invited to contemplate the mysteries of fate, the challenges of mid-life crisis, the beauty of nature and the seasons, the solace of the human spirit, and the ongoing journey of self-discovery. With wisdom and insight, this collection of eighty reflections invites us to contemplate the depths of our humanity and to celebrate the power of the human spirit to persevere and to grow."

With love and gratitude,

The 'Homo Sapiens' Series Team"

Acknowledgements

This book is a testament to the timeless exploration of the human condition and the ever-evolving journey of self-discovery. The author, Mawphniang Napoleon, masterfully employs the art of poetry to delve into the depths of human emotions, experiences, and perspectives. Each reflection offers a unique and profound insight into the complexities of being human, reminding us of our shared experiences, struggles, and triumphs.

As we embark on this journey through the pages of this book, we are reminded of the significance of introspection, self-reflection, and contemplation in shaping our understanding of humanity. It is through these poetic reflections that we gain a deeper appreciation for the intricacies of our existence and the boundless potential for growth and self-awareness.

We are grateful to the author for sharing this collection with the world, and we hope that readers will find comfort, solace, and inspiration in its pages. May this book serve as a reminder of the beauty and wonder of human life and our never-ending quest for knowledge and understanding.

As we delve into each poem, we are transported to new realms of thought, where we question the very fabric of our being and the world around us. Mawphniang Napoleon's words are a testament to the power of language to evoke emotions, spark new ideas, and stimulate our imagination.

This book is not just a collection of poems, but a philosophical journey that challenges us to rethink our preconceived notions of humanity and our place in the world. It is a reminder that we are all connected by our shared experiences and emotions, and that our humanity transcends all borders and boundaries.

As we close the final page, we are left with a renewed appreciation for the beauty of humanity, and the endless possibilities that lie ahead. This book is a tribute to the human spirit, and a call to action for us to continue our journey of self-discovery and growth.

We acknowledge the profound impact that this book will have on its readers, and we express our deepest gratitude to Mawphniang Napoleon for his contribution to the philosophical discourse on humanity.

With love and gratitude,

The 'Homo Sapiens' Series Team"

Prologue

This book, Homo Sapiens Part – XI, is a testament to the power of reflection and introspection. The author, Mawphniang Napoleon, invites us on a journey through a collection of eighty poems, each exploring a different facet of humanity. Through examining themes such as fate, mid-life crisis, nature and seasons, solace, and self-discovery, the author invites us to consider the human experience from a multitude of perspectives.

This collection serves as a reminder of the universality of human experience and the power of language to bring us together in understanding. Whether it is through the lyrical beauty of the words or the profound insight into the human condition, these poems invite us to contemplate our place in the world and the meaning of our existence.

It is not enough to simply exist in the world, but to truly live, we must engage in self-reflection and seek to understand the complexities of our own humanity. This book is a call to action, a reminder that our journey through life is one of constant growth and discovery.

So, as you delve into this collection of poetic reflections, we invite you to embrace the power of introspection and to explore the depths of your own humanity. And, do not forget to read other books in the same series and other works by the same author, as they will surely deepen your understanding and appreciation of the human experience.

With love and gratitude,

The 'Homo Sapiens' Series Team"

1. The Ebb and Flow of Nature's Rhythms

The wistful winds of change doth blow,
And nature's cycle doth unfold;
From winter's chill to summer's glow,
The seasons shift, their stories told
In colors of the leaves that show
The passage of the years untold.

With every fall, the leaves do turn
From hues of green to shades of gold,
And with the chill, they gently burn
In flickers of the autumn cold.
And as they fall, they doth return
To earth, a cycle to uphold.

The springtime brings new life anew,
With buds that burst in shades of green,
And with the rain, they gently grew,
And nature's beauty is serene.
And summer brings its scorching hue,
With warmth that nurtures all, unseen.

But as the summer starts to fade,
And autumn breezes blow once more,
The cycle starts anew, displayed

In colors of the leaves that pour
From trees in hues of orange, red,
And brown, a symphony to adore.

And as the winter comes in sight,
And frosty winds begin to blow,
The trees are stripped of their delight,
And nature takes a restful bow.
But with the spring, they take to flight,
And new beginnings start to grow.

Thus nature's cycle doth repeat,
With changing seasons at its core,
And though its rhythms may seem fleet,
Its beauty shall forever soar.
For every year, with every beat,
It shall forever be adored.

And as the cycle spins on, we find
The mystery of nature, vast and grand,
And every season of the mind,
A manifestation of a cosmic hand,
That weaves its magic, intertwined,
With all the forces of the land.

The universe, with all its power,
Is but a mere reflection of the grace
That lies within each fleeting hour,
A dance of life, with time and space.

And so, with every changing hour,
The seasons come, and pass without trace.

The autumn winds, they call us forth,
To heed the siren's mournful cry,
And beckon us to leave the North,
And venture to the bygone sky.
And in that sky, we find the worth,
Of life and death, and reasons why.

The winter brings its frosty chill,
And paints the earth in shades of white,
A world transformed, a crystal still,
That echoes with a distant light.
And in that light, we see the thrill,
Of nature's secrets, cryptic, bright.

And as the springtime starts to bloom,
The world awakens from its slumber,
And every blossom spells a doom,
For all the beauty that it encumbers.
And yet, we see a brighter room,
With hope and joy, a constant number.

And summer brings its scorching blaze,
And bathes the earth in light divine,
A symphony of fire and rays,
That dances in a cosmic line.
And in that line, we find the ways,

Of life and death, a sacred sign.

Thus, nature's cycle doth remain,
A dance of life, with no end in sight,
A journey that will always sustain,
With every change, a new delight.
And so, we embrace the change,
And find our place, in this cosmic light.

And as we journey through life's seas,
We find the truth of nature's song,
A tale of wonder, mysteries,
That echoes in our hearts, so strong.
And though we may not comprehend,
The secrets that it holds, so long.

The changing seasons, they remind,
Of nature's power, so profound,
A rhythm that is hard to find,
But always present, all around.
And so we seek, with eager mind,
To unravel nature's mystery, unwound.

The autumn leaves, they swirl and spin,
In colors of the setting sun,
And as they fall, they teach within,
The lessons of the journey begun.
And in that journey, we begin,
To see the wonders that we've won.

The winter's frost, it brings such peace,
A world of stillness, calm and cold,
And as we bask in its release,
We find a story, yet untold.
And in that story, we find the keys,
To unlock nature's secrets, bold.

The springtime brings new life once more,
With buds that burst in shades of green,
And with the rain, they gently pour,
And nature's beauty is serene.
And summer brings its scorching roar,
With warmth that nurtures all, serene.

And so the cycle doth repeat,
With changing seasons at its core,
And though its rhythms may be fleet,
Its beauty shall forever more.
For every year, with every beat,
Nature's cycle shall forever soar.

And yet, amidst this grand parade,
We find that nature's gifts are not
For us to take, but to be made,
A part of, in a sacred knot.
For we are but mere agents, played
In nature's symphony, begot.

The autumn winds, they swirl and sway,
In gusts that sweep across the land,
And though they may strip trees away,
They bring a richness, oh so grand.
And in that richness, we portray,
The beauty of life, that's in our hand.

The winter's snow, it falls so still,
And wraps the earth in shimmering white,
A world of peace, where all is still,
And nature whispers in the night.
And in that night, we find the thrill,
Of secrets kept, beyond our sight.

The springtime brings new life to birth,
With blooms that paint the earth so bright,
And in that light, we see the worth,
Of nature's gifts, that fill our sight.
And summer brings its scorching mirth,
With warmth that enlivens, day and night.

Thus, nature's cycle doth persist,
With seasons that come and go,
A dance of life, that cannot resist,
The cosmic forces that we know.
And though we may not understand,
The secrets that it holds, so grand.

So let us bask in nature's light,

And revel in its wondrous ways,
And though its rhythms may not be bright,
Its beauty shall forever blaze.
For in its cycle, we take flight,
And find a home, in nature's gaze.

And as we stand amidst the fray,
Of life's tumultuous, endless tides,
We find that nature lights the way,
And guides us on our wondrous rides.
For in its cycle, we can say,
That we have found a place to reside.

The autumn winds, they sing and play,
A melody, so rich and bright,
And though they may bring pain, we sway,
And find a solace, in their light.
And in that light, we find a way,
To heal our wounds, with nature's might.

The winter's frost, it glistens bright,
With icicles, that gleam and glow,
And in its beauty, we take flight,
To realms, beyond what we may know.
And though its chill may cause fright,
It brings a peace, that will not go.

The springtime brings new life once more,
With buds that burst in shades of green,

And with the rain, they gently pour,
And nature's beauty is serene.
And summer brings its scorching roar,
With warmth that nurtures all, serene.

Thus, nature's cycle doth repeat,
With seasons that come and go,
A dance of life, that cannot be beat,
With secrets, that we may not know.
And though we may not comprehend,
The ways of nature, to the end.

So let us embrace the mystery,
Of nature's changing seasons, dear,
And though its secrets may not be,
For us to know, they still are near.
For in its cycle, we shall see,
The beauty that is always here.

And as we journey through life's quest,
We find that nature is our guide,
A beacon of light, that does its best,
To show us beauty, far and wide.
For in its cycle, we find rest,
And solace in its peaceful tide.

The autumn winds, they howl and sing,
A song of change, that is so grand,
And though they may bring destruction's sting,

They bring new growth, with gentle hand.
And in that growth, we find a fling,
Of joy, that doth expand.

The winter's snow, it falls so slow,
And covers all, in a pure sheet,
And in its silence, we doth grow,
And find a peace, that cannot be beat.
And though its grip may make us glow,
It brings a beauty, that's unique.

The springtime brings new life anew,
With sprouts that reach for sun and sky,
And in its promise, we find a view,
Of endless possibilities, that lie.
And summer brings its scorching hue,
With warmth that doth not say goodbye.

Thus, nature's cycle doth remain,
With seasons that come and go,
A dance of life, that cannot be feigned,
With secrets, that we may not know.
And though we may not comprehend,
The ways of nature, to the end.

So let us celebrate its grace,
And revel in its wondrous show,
And though its rhythm may not pace,
Its beauty shall forever grow.

For in its cycle, we find place,
And peace, that shall forever flow.

And as we journey through life's maze,
We find that nature is our ally,
A gentle guide, that shows us ways,
To beauty, that doth not pall or fall away.
For in its cycle, we find daze,
And wonder, that shall not decay.

The autumn leaves, they swirl and dance,
In colors bright, that are so rare,
And though they may bring chance,
They bring new life, that we should care.
And in that care, we find a glance,
Of joy, that shines beyond compare.

The winter's snow, it falls so fast,
And covers all, in a blanket white,
And in its stillness, we are cast,
Into a peace, that cannot be quite.
And though its grip may not last,
It brings a calm, that shines so bright.

The springtime brings new hope once more,
With buds that burst, in shades of green,
And in its promise, we find a roar,
Of endless possibilities, that have been seen.
And summer brings its scorching store,

With warmth that nurtures all, serene.

Thus, nature's cycle doth endure,
With seasons that come and go,
A dance of life, that shall ensure,
Its secrets, that we may never know.
And though we may not comprehend,
The ways of nature, to the end.

So let us bask in nature's light,
And find its beauty in each day,
And though its path may not be right,
Its wonders shall never go away.
For in its cycle, we find might,
And peace, that shall forever stay.

And as we traverse life's winding road,
We find that nature is our guide,
A source of comfort, that doth bestow,
A beauty, that cannot be denied.
For in its cycle, we find a flow,
Of serenity, that shall not subside.

The autumn rains, they come with might,
And wash away, the summer's dust,
And though they may bring a frightening sight,
They bring renewal, that we must trust.
And in that trust, we find delight,
In nature's cycle, that is just.

The winter's frost, it bites so deep,
And turns the world, into a wonderland,
And in its stillness, we do keep,
A peace, that cannot be forced to bend.
And though its grip may make us sleep,
It brings a beauty, that cannot be penned.

The springtime brings new life to all,
With flowers that bloom, in radiant hues,
And in their promise, we do call,
For endless possibilities, that ensue.
And summer brings its scorching hall,
With warmth that doth renew.

Thus, nature's cycle doth persist,
With seasons that come and go,
A dance of life, that shall not miss,
Its secrets, that we may never know.
And though we may not comprehend,
The ways of nature, to the end.

So let us revel in nature's grace,
And find its beauty, in each moment,
And though its path may not have pace,
Its wonders shall always be augment.
For in its cycle, we find space,
And peace, that shall forever augment.

And as we navigate life's winding path,
We find that nature is our ally,
A solace in our moments of wrath,
A beauty, that cannot be vilified.
For in its cycle, we find a balm,
Of serenity, that shall not ebb away.

The autumn winds, they come with gale,
And sweep away, the summer's heat,
And though they may bring a fearsome trail,
They bring a cooling, that is a treat.
And in that treat, we find a veil,
Of peace, that cannot be incomplete.

The winter's ice, it glistens bright,
And turns the world, into a crystal wonder,
And in its stillness, we do ignite,
A sense of awe, that cannot be sunder.
And though its grip may be in sight,
It brings a serenity, that cannot be blunder.

The springtime brings new hope once more,
With blossoms that bloom, in fragrant air,
And in their promise, we restore,
A sense of joy, that is beyond compare.
And summer brings its scorching roar,
With warmth that doth repair.

Thus, nature's cycle doth ensconce,

With seasons that come and go,
A dance of life, that shall not douse,
Its secrets, that we may never know.
And though we may not comprehend,
The ways of nature, to the end.

So let us bask in nature's light,
And find its beauty, in each day,
And though its path may not be in sight,
Its wonders shall always be at bay.
For in its cycle, we find might,
And peace, that shall forever stay.

2. The Ephemeral Dance with Time

To contemplate or retrogress to a prior subject,
Is but a reminiscence of our ephemeral fate.
Time, a despotic ruler, never to abstain,
And events, but a cyclicality of enmity.

We attempt to comprehend what is evanescent,
But it eludes us like granules of sand.
The past, a reminiscence, forever evanescent,
Leaving us with naught but empty palms.

We yearn for a return to more unassuming ages,
But it's a chimerical pursuit, my dear.
For time is a stream, ever flowing,
And we, but mere receptacles, ever in trepidation.

We are but mere puppets, controlled by fate,
Destined to reiterate the same errors.
Our existence, but a transient state,
And all our attempts, but chimerical ruptures.

So let us not contemplate or retrogress,
But submit to our fate, and let time kindle.

And in submission, let us find solace,

In the realization that all is fleeting.
For though our lives are but a mere trifle,
They hold within them meaning, profound and fleeting.

Let us embrace the fleeting nature of life,
And in its transience, find beauty and grace.
For though time may be a ruthless sovereign,
It is also a teacher, leading us to a higher place.

In the face of adversity, let us be resolute,
And in the face of loss, let us find acceptance.
For all that we hold dear is but a moment,
And in its passing, we find a greater sense.

So let us not lament the passing of time,
But rather, let us cherish each fleeting moment divine.
For in the grand scheme of things, it is but a mere chime,
But a chime that echoes through eternity, in the hearts of those who find.

So let us make the most of our time,
And in its fleetingness, find purpose and drive.
Let us leave behind a legacy,
That echoes through the ages, long after we've died.

For though our bodies may wither and fade,
Our deeds, forever remain.
In the hearts of those we've touched, we'll never fade,
Our memory, a guiding light, forever to sustain.

So let us not squander our time in despair,
But rather, let us make our mark, and leave a trace.
For though our time on earth may be scarce,
Our impact, forever etched in the annals of time and space.

So let us embrace the fleeting nature of life,
And in its transience, find meaning and strive.
For though time may be a ruthless sovereign,
It is also a gift, and we should make the most of it, while alive.

3. The Mortal's Plea: In Search of Solace

In times of melancholy, when the night doth linger,

And all around is shrouded in darkness, and hope is evanescent,

We turn to supplication, to seek a transcendent power,

To guide us through the ordeals of the present moment.

But what if faith, that panacea for despair,

Has been impaired, and we find no solace

From any divinity, or supernal force,

That once brought us some modicum of remorse?

We are but mere mortals, feeble and fragile,

With no agency over our own destiny,

And though we implore and entreat to no avail,

We are but marionettes in a cosmic spectacle.

So let us not in vain seek aid above,

For in this world, we are but fated to love.

4. A Timid Heart's Remembrance

On that fateful day, when in the hall of academia,

I chanced upon thy visage, and was filled with ecstasy,

Thy bashfulness and rosy hue, did catch my gaze,

And though my own tongue was tied, in shyness' daze.

I feared to speak, lest my words should be inane,

For where I hailed, my manner was deemed demure,

But still, thy smile, so fair and sweet, doth remain,

Thy countenance, aesthetically pure.

These memories, now years hence, yet linger still,

The aroma of Doh Jem, a savory delight,

But all I could behold, was thy visage, so shrill,

And my own timidity, did bar my tongue from flight.

Though I never mustered the courage to speak,

Thy beauty and thy smile, forever, in my mind, shall be etched.

5. Melancholy's Journey: A Quest for Self-Discovery and Transcendence

With inordinate fervor, I hasten forth
Towards melancholy's gloomy, dark embrace
A fervent rush to feel the sorrows spawn
And bask within the shadows of that place

But why do I, with such alacrity, run
Towards sadness, as if it were a boon
Why seek to wallow in the setting sun
When I could bask in beams of golden dune

Perhaps it is the pain that calls to me
The whisper of the broken heart's despair
A siren song that I cannot but hear
And rush towards, though I know it's not fair

But still, I hasten towards the melancholy
For in its depths, I find my solace to be.

Yet in this solace, lies a bitter truth
That all our joys and hopes, in time, will cease
The world a stage for misery and ruth
And we but actors in the grand decease

But in this sorrow, there is also beauty
A reminder of our fleeting mortality
For in the end, it is this pain that makes us see
The preciousness of life, and its fragility

So let us rush towards sorrow's bitter kiss
For in its arms, we find true meaning, in this.

And though the journey may be arduous,
With moments of despair and hopelessness,
I know that in this melancholy, there is a spark,
That will guide me to the light, and true consciousness.

For in the quest for self-discovery,
I must delve deep into the shadows of my mind,
And confront the demons and insecurities,
That have been holding me back, all this time.

But with each step, I gain new insight,
And understanding of my very essence,
And in this, I find my true might,
To transcend the sorrows, with persistence.

For the melancholy, is not just a prison,
But a gateway to true understanding,
And in this quest, I find true wisdom,
And the power to transcend, my own suffering.

And as I journey on this path,
Of self-discovery and transcendence,
I know that in the melancholy, the aftermath,
Will be a true understanding of my existence.

For in this quest, I shall find my true self,
And the purpose that I was meant to fulfill,
And in this, I shall find my true wealth,
A true understanding of my melancholy's will.

And though the journey may be long,
And the path may be difficult to tread,
I know that in the melancholy, there is a song,
That will guide me, till the end.

For in this quest, I shall find my true self,
And the beauty that lies within the sorrow,
And in this, I shall find my true wealth,
A true understanding, for tomorrow.

So let me not be held captive,
By the sorrows that may assail,
For in the quest for self-discovery, I shall strive,
And transcend the limitations, that may veil.

6. The Chic Deception: A Portrait of a Rapscallion

A rapscallion, so urbane in his habiliment,
A mountebank, with no scruple or sentiment.
An unprincipled knave, who preys on the infirm,
A petty malefactor, whose ethics are squirm.

His chic raiment masks the putrefaction within,
A veneer of propriety, but nothing to win.
His orations are mellifluous, but his actions are noisome,
A serpent in the herbage, with nothing to gloating.

He traverses life, with a sly, contorted smirk,
A virtuoso of deception, who will not berk.
His sole objective, is to acquire what he can,
And leave desolation in his path, like a man.

But in the end, his destiny is sealed,
For all his wealth, his psyche will be revealed.
A genuine mirror of his inner self,
A petty malefactor, with nothing to tell.

His chic habiliment and mellifluous orations, a masquerade,
A mere visor for the iniquity that lurks inside.

7. Delectable Jadoh of Iewduh: A Culinary Ode to Homesickness

Amidst the realm of gastronomic delights,
There doth exist a dish of such great might
That, once tasted, doth leave the tongue beguiled
And in the mind, memories long enshrined

Delectable Jadoh of Iewduh, a repast
That doth the senses with its essence cast
A symphony of flavors, both robust
And savory, a culinary delight that doth

The palate with its delectable embrace
Nourish both body and soul, a true grace
Jadoh Snam, a delicacy of the Khasi race
A harmonious blend of pork and blood, with rice of hued

But as I yearn for Jadoh in my stomach's core
I find myself in a state of melancholic lure
The thought of Jadoh, a solace and a warmth, once more
To my longing for my natal territory

So let me savor every morsel slow
And find in food a deeper, truer glow

A reminder of home, a culinary treasure
A gastronomic pleasure beyond measure.

But as I indulge in this delectable fare,
I am reminded of a deeper truth to bear
The sustenance of the body is not all,
But also the nourishment of the soul's call

For in the flavors and aromas of Jadoh,
I am reminded of my cultural heritage, a flow
Of tradition and history, a rich tapestry
That enriches not just my palate, but my identity

And thus, I am grateful for this humble dish
That not only satiates my physical wish,
But also feeds my soul and nourishes my mind
A culinary experience that is truly one of a kind

So let me savor every morsel with reverence
For in Jadoh, I find my cultural essence.

But as I delve deeper into the dish's story
I am confronted with a moral query
For in the preparation of Jadoh,
There is the taking of life, a sober

Reminder that sustenance comes at a cost
And in this, a balance must be sought
To honor and respect the life we consume

And to not let our appetites assume

A reckless and thoughtless path to satiety
But instead, to engage in a morality
Of conscious consumption, a mindful way
To nourish ourselves in a just and humane way

So let me savor every morsel with gratitude
For the gift of sustenance, and the responsibility it imbues.

And as I reflect upon this culinary art,
I am reminded of a deeper part
Of the human experience, the connection
Between sustenance and self-reflection

For in the enjoyment of Jadoh,
I am reminded of my place in the world and the roles
That food plays in our lives, not just sustenance,
But also community, culture, and existence

It is a reminder to be present in every bite
To savor the flavors, to appreciate the light
That shines through every dish, a reminder of the beauty
That surrounds us, if we only take the time to see

So let me savor every morsel with mindfulness
And find in food, a deeper sense of oneness.

And as I reach the end of this repast,

I am left with a sense of contentment and a sense of past
For in the enjoyment of Jadoh, I am reminded
Of the cyclical nature of life, and how all things are binded

The pig, whose life was taken for the dish
Will eventually become a part of the earth, to enrich
The soil and provide for future growth,
A reminder of the interconnectedness of all, a truth

So let me savor the last morsel with humility
For in this dish, I am reminded of my mortality
And the preciousness of life, a reminder to live each day
With gratitude, empathy, and in a mindful way.

And as I end this culinary journey,
I am left with a sense of epiphany
For in the enjoyment of Jadoh, I have come to realize
That food is not just sustenance, it's a celebration of life.
It's a way to connect with one's culture, tradition and history.
It's a way to nourish one's mind, body, and soul.
It's a way to appreciate the beauty of life, and the cycle of nature.
It's a way to cultivate mindfulness, empathy, and gratitude.

In this simple dish, I have found a deeper understanding
Of the complexities of life and the interconnectedness of all things.
I have come to realize that in every morsel, there is a story to be told
And in every meal, there is a deeper truth to be discovered.

So let me savor this experience with a profound appreciation

For the gift of food and the wisdom it holds, an inspiration.

Note :

Jadoh : Meghalayan equivalent of a pulao or biryani.

Iewduh : Heritage market in Shillong , Meghalaya

Khasi : Main tribe of Meghalaya , India

8. Eulogy for a Lost Light: Remembering Papa

As I sit here, feeling lost and alone,
I think back to the tales of old,
Of the great Russian writers,
Who knew the pain of grief and loss.

I think of Pushkin and his tragic love,
Of Dostoevsky and his struggles with faith,
I see my own pain reflected in their words,
And wonder if I will ever find peace.

The road ahead is long and winding,
With no guide to follow,
I am left to navigate this darkness,
With only my own regrets and sorrows.

I wish I could turn back time,
And see you one last time,
To tell you how much I love you,
And how much you meant to me.

But alas, it is too late,
You are gone and I am left,
To carry on in this dark world,
Without your light to guide me.

I am filled with regret and grief,
For the things left unsaid and undone,
I wish I could have made you proud,
But now I am left with only one.

The darkness surrounds me,
Like a cloak of despair,
As I try to make sense of the void,
That your absence has left in my life.

I often wonder, why you had to go,
Leaving me alone in this cruel world,
Did you not think of the pain I'd have to endure,
Or did you just not care?

Your absence leaves a gaping hole in my heart,
A void that can never be filled,
I miss your warmth and your love,
But all I have left are the memories of our time together.

I try to move on, to live my life,
But every day I am haunted by your ghost,
I see your face in every stranger,
Hoping that somehow you'll return to me.

But now, I am forced to carry on,
To live my life without you,
To face the challenges that come my way,

With a heavy heart and aching soul.

I try to find solace in the memories,
Of the good times we shared,
But the pain of your loss,
Is always there, like a constant reminder,
Of what could have been,
And what will never be.

I am left with a deep sense of regret,
Wondering if I could have done more,
To show you how much you meant to me,
Before it was too late.

But alas, you are gone forever,
Leaving me to mourn and grieve,
I am left with only regrets,
Wishing I could have done more for you.

I will always miss you, Papa,
You were the light in my life,
And now that you're gone, everything is dark and cold,
Leaving me with nothing but regret and sorrow

9. Cosmic Being: A Testimony of Strength and Uniqueness

Verily, a paradox of nature and fate,
Thou art a being of strength and uniqueness,
An enigma of power and spirit great,
A symbol of life's complex and harshness.

Thou art a prodigy of flesh and bone,
A masterpiece of genetic code,
A composition of cells and hormones,
A harmony of mind and soul bestowed.

Thou art a testament of time and space,
A chronicle of evolution's grace,
A milestone of conscious awareness,
A proof of existence's meaningful place.

Thou art a miracle of nature's will,
A mystery of divine and mortal skill.

Yet, despite thy strength and uniqueness,
Thou art but one among many, a piece
Of a puzzle, a part of a grand design,
A cosmic being in the universe align.

So, embrace thy strength and uniqueness,
And let thy spirit soar beyond the skies,
For thou art more than flesh and bone,
Thou art a star, a light that never dies.

Thou art the essence of existence's quest,
A human being, a part of the divine,
A soul that's meant to seek and manifest,
A journey that's always yours to shine.

Thus, embrace thy strength and uniqueness,
And seek the truth that lies within thee,
For thou art a being of such greatness,
A vessel of power, wisdom, and beauty.

Thou art a warrior of thy own fate,
A conqueror of life's many battles,
A fighter for what is truly great,
A hero of this world's endless struggles.

Thou art a beacon of hope and love,
A source of inspiration for many,
A lighthouse of guidance from above,
A reminder of the power of unity.

Thou art a scholar of the unknown,
A master of knowledge, reason, and thought,
A seeker of the mysteries yet shown,

A champion of wisdom, logic, and naught.

Thou art a unique and strong human being,
A force of nature, a symbol of divinity,
Thou art a part of this world's soul,
A spirit that will always be set free.

So, embrace thy strength and uniqueness,
And let thy journey be an endless quest,
For thou art a being of great power,
A light that will forever shine and bless.

And as thou travels on this life's path,
Remember that thy strength is not alone,
For thou art but a fraction of a whole,
A part of a great, universal tone.

Thy uniqueness is not a solitary trait,
But a facet of a larger tapestry,
A stitch in a grand, cosmic creation,
A beauty that the universe can see.

So, let thy strength and uniqueness shine,
And share it with the world in its need,
For thy light can brighten many a life,
And bring hope to those who're lost in deed.

For thou art not just a human being,
But a messenger of love and hope,

A harbinger of change and freedom,
A voice of truth that helps to cope.

And in this knowledge, thou shall find,
A reason to embrace thy strength and grace,
For thou art a unique and strong human being,
A symbol of life's beauty and its pace.

And so, my friend, let not the world's woes
Dim the brilliance of thy shining light,
For thou art a source of hope and joy,
A beacon of truth that shines so bright.

Let not the trials and tribulations
Take away thy strength and beauty's grace,
For thou art a force to be reckoned with,
A spirit that defies all limitations.

And when the winds of change do howl and roar,
And life's challenges seek to break thee down,
Remember that thou art not alone,
That thou hast strength that can wear the crown.

For thou art a unique and strong human being,
A creature of might, grace, and resilience,
A symbol of life's boundless possibilities,
A testament of the human spirit's excellence.

So, embrace thy strength and uniqueness,

And let thy journey be a path of light,
For thou art a being of great power,
A shining star in this world's endless night.

And as thou walks this life's winding road,
Remember to keep thy focus true,
For the journey ahead is long and bold,
And the challenges thou wilt face anew.

But with thy strength and uniqueness,
Thou can overcome any obstacle,
And rise above the challenges at hand,
To reach the summit of thy noble goal.

For thou art a master of thy own fate,
A conqueror of life's many battles,
A fighter for what is truly great,
A hero of this world's endless struggles.

And in thy journey, thou shall find,
The meaning and purpose of thy life,
The reason for the challenges thou hast faced,
And the wisdom that shall end the strife.

So, embrace thy strength and uniqueness,
And let thy journey be an endless quest,
For thou art a being of great power,
A light that will forever shine and bless.

And as thou travels further down the road,
Let not the fear of failure hold thee back,
For thou hast the power to overcome,
And achieve great things with every track.

For thou art a unique and strong human being,
A creature of unbreakable resolve,
A master of thy own destiny,
A spirit that shall always evolve.

And when the doubts and insecurities
Seek to bring thee down in despair,
Remember that thou art more than this,
And that thou hast a soul that doth repair.

For thou art a light that shines so bright,
A source of hope and inspiration,
A reminder of the power of love,
A symbol of life's sweet adoration.

So, embrace thy strength and uniqueness,
And let thy journey be a path of light,
For thou art a being of great power,
A shining star in this world's endless night.

And as thou stands amidst the raging storm,
With courage in thy heart and fire in thy soul,
Remember that thou art not alone,
That thou hast a strength that makes thee whole.

For thou art a unique and strong human being,
A creature of resilience and determination,
A master of thy own thoughts and feelings,
A spirit that defies all explanation.

And in the face of life's great unknown,
Thou must trust in thy own inner guide,
For it is the voice of thy own soul,
A voice that shall never be denied.

So, embrace thy strength and uniqueness,
And let thy journey be an endless quest,
For thou art a being of great power,
A light that will forever shine and bless.

For thou art a unique and strong human being,
A symbol of life's boundless possibilities,
A source of hope and inspiration,
A testament of the human spirit's capabilities.

And as thou stands on the brink of change,
With doubts and fears both close at hand,
Remember that thou art the master,
And that thou hast the power to command.

For thou art a unique and strong human being,
A creature of unwavering conviction,
A master of thy own thoughts and actions,

A spirit of boundless intuition.

And in the face of life's great challenge,
Thou must have faith in thy own abilities,
For thou hast the strength to overcome,
And reach the summit of life's realities.

So, embrace thy strength and uniqueness,
And let thy journey be an endless quest,
For thou art a being of great power,
A light that will forever shine and bless.

For thou art a unique and strong human being,
A symbol of hope and resilience,
A source of courage and inspiration,
A testament of the human spirit's existence.

10. The Junk Food Plague: A Sonnet on Healthy Eating

In modern times, junk food doth prevail,
A diet rich in sugar, salt, and fat.
It tempts the taste buds with each tasty tale,
And health is oft neglected in its grasp.

The body cries for nourishment pure,
Yet junk doth fill the stomach to the brim.
Its addictive taste, a subtle allure,
That makes one ignore the harm it may bring.

The grease and preservatives do impart,
A slow and steady toll upon the frame.
The veins and arteries, they do start,
To harden and constrict, 'til health is lame.

The food we eat, it is the very fuel,
That drives the engine of our mortal coil.
If junk is all we choose to ingest,
Our bodies shall be plagued with ailments worst.

Thus, let us be mindful of our diets,
And choose the foods that make our bodies thrive.
For health, it is the key to long-lived,
And junk food, it is the quick road to dive.

So let us take the path of wisdom's light,
And nourish our bodies with foods that heal.
For health, it is a precious precious sight,
And junk food, it is the root of ill.

So sayeth I, with wisdom and with rhyme,
Let us forsake the junk and eat divine.
And may we all, in perfect health, climb,
To the summit of our lives, in good time.

But ah, to many, junk food is a treat,
A source of comfort in their daily life.
It numbs the pain and calms the inner heat,
And offers solace from the daily strife.

Yet still, the toll it takes on health so dear,
Is like a ticking time bomb in the soul.
For it doth cause disease and bring forth tear,
And steals away the joys that make us whole.

So let us be aware, and make a choice,
To shun the junk and seek what's truly wise.
For health is wealth, and cannot be replaced,
And junk food is the thief that steals it twice.

In every meal, the power lies in us,
To choose the path that leads to health and trust.
And though the junk may taste so sweet and just,

Its harm doth far outweigh the moment's lust.

So let us be wise, and choose aright,
And nourish bodies with what's pure and bright.
For health is the foundation of life's might,
And junk food, it is the cause of night.

Not to end this sonnet, with any final word,
A call to arms, to make a change in diet.
For health is the most precious gift we've earned,
And junk food, it is the thing we should avoid

And as we make this choice, so shall we find,
The power to heal and to grow strong.
The body shall thrive, the spirit shall unwind,
And we shall live our lives, the whole day long.

For health is not a destination, nay,
But a journey, that we undertake.
With every meal, we shape our future way,
And choose the path, that shall our lives make.

And so, let us be mindful of our choice,
And choose the foods that make our bodies shine.
For health is wealth, beyond all other joys,
And junk food, it is the foe of thine.

So let us take the path that leads to light,
And nourish our bodies, with what's pure and bright.

And may we live, with health and strength in sight,
And revel in the joys, of life's delight.

And so, In this sonnet, with a bow,
And leave you with a final thought in mind.
That health is yours, to shape and to bestow,
And junk food, it is a curse, you'll find.

So choose with care, each meal and every bite,
And let your health be your utmost prize.
For what we eat, it shapes our future's light,
And junk food, it is the shadow in disguise.

It saps our strength, it dulls our mental might,
And steals away the joys that life can bring.
It robs us of the power to take flight,
And leaves us weak, in body, mind and spirit.

So let us rise, and make a change today,
And choose the foods that nourish and sustain.
For health is more than wealth, in every way,
And junk food, it is a curse, in vain.

And as we walk this path, so shall we see,
The power that good health can bring to thee.
With every meal, we shall be free,
And live our lives, with strength and liberty.

So be of good cheer, and take this sonnet's cue,

And choose the path that leads to health and truth.
For junk food is a trap, it's false and untrue,
And health is yours, to claim and hold and use.

And as we make this choice, so shall we find,
A life of joy, and peace, and happiness.
The body shall prosper, the mind shall unwind,
And we shall bask, in health's warm caress.

For health is not a destination, nay,
But a journey, that we undertake.
With every meal, we shape our future way,
And choose the path, that shall our lives make.

And so, let us be steadfast in our goal,
And nourish our bodies, with what's true and right.
For health is the foundation of our soul,
And junk food, it is the source of night.

And as we walk this path, so shall we grow,
In strength, and wisdom, and in grace divine.
For health is a treasure, that we bestow,
And junk food, it is a burden, that we decline.

And so, I end this sonnet, with a smile,
And leave you with a final thought so wise.
That health is yours, to keep, and all the while,
And junk food, it is a choice, you'll realize.

• 45 •

11. Solitude: A Friend for the Journey

Solitude, my dear friend,
I find myself seeking you again and again.
In the quiet moments of contemplation,
You bring a sense of peace and understanding.

Your presence allows me to ponder
The mysteries of life and the world around me.
To delve deep into my own thoughts and feelings,
To uncover the truths that lie within.

With you by my side, I am free
To explore my own path, to chart my own course.
I am not held back by the opinions of others,
But instead, I am guided by my own inner compass.

Solitude, you are a gift,
A chance to reconnect with myself and my purpose.
You offer a chance to slow down,
To breathe, to think, to be.

So I embrace you, dear solitude,
As a dear and trusted friend.
For in your embrace, I find the strength
To face whatever challenges life may bring.

12. The Path of Contemplation: A Journey to Inner Peace

Contemplation, a beauty so divine
A state of mind, a peaceful design
A path to enlightenment, a way to transcend
The ego's grasp, a journey to befriend

The present moment, a gift to behold
A chance to find peace, a story to be told
To let go of fear, and embrace the unknown
To embrace the present, and let go of the groan

The beauty of contemplation, a treasure to seek
A way to find balance, and inner peace speak
A path to wisdom, a way to be free
From the chains of the past, and the burden of gree

It is a journey, a path to be trod
A way to find clarity, a path to God
A way to find meaning, and purpose anew
In the beauty of contemplation, a journey to pursue

So let us embrace, this gift of the mind
And find peace within, and leave worry behind

For in the beauty of contemplation, we will find
A path to enlightenment, and peace of mind.

13. Small Chats, Big Impact: The Beauty of Human Connection

The absurdity of small talk,
Why bother with a stranger in a crowded place?
We have too much to do and friends to see,
Why waste our time with idle chatter?

We aspire to be profound,
To have deep and meaningful conversations.
But perhaps we are missing the point,
Of the beauty in the small and insignificant.

For in these fleeting moments,
We connect with another human being.
We share a moment of humanity,
In a world that can often feel cold and impersonal.

Minor social exchanges, small chats and kind words,
Can carry more weight than lengthy friendships and novels.
A single sentence can mark us, a picture can stick with us,
In ways that a three hour film never could.

We are all so close to sadness, to self-hatred and regret,
A short exchange can turn around a dark day.

Compressed in the smallest of dialogues,
Sympathy and fellow-feeling can be found.

"They make them like that to torture us, don't they?"
A simple statement of understanding, of shared struggle.
In these minor exchanges, we find solace,
A reminder that we are not alone in this world.

As we go about our daily lives,
We never truly know what lies within.
The struggles, the pain, the thoughts of despair,
That haunt those we encounter everywhere.

But a simple exchange, a few sympathetic words,
Can make a world of difference to those who are hurting.
A moment of humanity, a display of hope,
Might be the last thing between someone and despair.

We can never know for certain, as Schopenhauer said,
Who around us may be thinking of ending their own life.
But we can choose to be kind, to offer a listening ear,
To show that we care and that they are not alone in their strife.

So let's strive to be better, to offer a helping hand,
To those who are struggling, to show them they matter.
For in every exchange, there may be much at stake,
And we have the power to bring hope and joy, rather than shatter.

In small chats, we connect with another soul,

Despite the barriers of distance and time.
We may not know the details of their lives,
But our hearts go out to them all the same.

We can imagine their pains and struggles,
And feel a deep sense of love and care.
It may seem paradoxical,
But we can love a stranger, even for just a moment.

This is the beauty of human connection,
The ability to feel and empathize with others.
In small chats and fleeting encounters,
We find a sense of humanity and belonging.

So let us not dismiss the power of small chats,
For they can bring us closer to each other,
Bonding us in a way that is pure and true,
A love that transcends the boundaries of time and space.

We often aim too high,
Thinking we must change the world,
But we forget the small things,
The power that lies within our hands.

We are assembled out of small things,
A warm hello, a sympathetic smile,
These may seem insignificant,
But they can make a world of difference.

So let us not neglect the power we hold,

To make a positive impact right now,

In the present moment,

For it is in these small acts that significance lies.

14. Breaking the Chains: Overcoming Addiction through Self-Reflection and Compassion

Addiction consumes us, consuming our time and energy,
Harming ourselves and neglecting our true interests.
Bulimia, porn addiction, and alcoholism,
All destructive behaviours we find hard to resist.

But there is a way to break the cycle,
To notice the desire before it consumes us whole.
To look within ourselves and understand,
The root of the pain that drives us to this self-harm.

Triggers vary, but they all stem from emotions deep within,
Loneliness, shame, rejection, a feeling of not being good enough.
Addiction is a response to pain we cannot understand or address,
A temporary escape from an unbearable discomfort.

But we can slow down the process,
Realize we are in trouble, feeling sad and hopeless.
We can observe our moods and put a gap between the pain and the solution.
Wake ourselves up from the narcotic impulse and say, "I am upset."

Ask ourselves the important questions, "What am I upset about? How am I upset?"
We can offer ourselves self-compassion and understanding,
Replacing addiction with love and care for ourselves.
It's never too late to heal and break the cycle of addiction.

15. Cosmic Dust: Embracing Our Power in a Vast Universe

We are but fleeting specks
In a vast and endless cosmos
Our lives but a moment's pause
Between the grand scale of gluons
And the infinite expanse of galaxies

We are but dust and stardust
Forged in the fiery furnace of creation
Yet we dream and desire
As if we had some great purpose
In this universe of impartial laws

We are but passionate pawns
In the hands of grand-master chance
Our will and wishes
But a mere whisper in the wind
As we watch the world spin
Counter to our desires
And ourselves bend
Against our own will

Yet even as we struggle
Against the forces that shape us
We are alive, and that is enough

To keep on dreaming, to keep on fighting
For a future that is yet unwritten
In this strange and wondrous world.

Against the vastness of the universe,
Our sense of self seems small and fragile.
How can we find the strength to rise up,
And embrace the power of our own will?

In this grand and unforgiving expanse,
We are but specks of dust, adrift and lost.
Yet, we seek to fill our lives with meaning,
To find purpose in the chaos and the fray.

But how, against the backdrop of this cosmic helplessness,
Can we muster the sense of agency necessary
To live our lives with purpose and with grace?
To find the majesty in every day?

Perhaps it lies within ourselves,
The courage and the strength to carry on,
To face the world with open hearts and minds,
To find the beauty and the joy within.

Our everyday gestures,
Though seemingly small and mundane,
Have consequences far beyond our understanding,
Rippling out through time and space.

We may feel insignificant,
But our actions have meaning,
They burst the seams of our intent,
Spilling forth with purpose and impact.

We are not nothing,
Our deeds are replete with significance,
Changing the world in ways we may never know.

So let us embrace the miraculous,
In every heartbeat, every breath,
And live with intention,
Knowing that our actions matter.

We are all so much more
Than we give ourselves credit for
Our actions, big or small
Can create a ripple effect, that's sure

We have the power to shape the world
To make a positive change
But it's up to us to take that chance
To stand up and make a difference, to arrange

We are not impotent or useless
But rather, we are dynamic
Exquisitely and frighteningly so
We have a duty to take responsibility
To not let our potential go

Our most ordinary and urgent duty
Is to embrace our power and use it right
To create a world that is better for all
We must stand up, take responsibility, and fight.

16. The Nourishment of Knowledge: The Power of What Thou Eateth and Readeth

Verily, thou art what thou eateth and what thou readeth
For in thy food and in thy books, doth shape thy being
In the inner depths of thy soul, doth they bring
The wisdom and the knowledge, that to thee, doth sing.

As the grains of wheat and the seeds of corn
Are ground into flour, and then made into bread,
So too is the knowledge, which thou taketh in
Transformed, to create the essence of thy mind.

And as the body is built from what it feedeth on,
So too is the soul, from what thou readeth.
Words, written by those who have come before,
Do shape the fabric of thy thoughts, for ever more.

For each page thou turneth, doth bring a new insight,
Each chapter a different perspective to thee,
And as thou delve deeper, into the book's lore,
Thou dost find the truth, of what it really means.

And thus, thou must choose, what thou wishest to eat,
For as the body is strengthened by its food,
So too is the soul, by what thou readeth.
Therefore, be careful, in what thou feedeth thy mind.

For the knowledge of the world, can be both true and false,
And if thou art not cautious, thou may be led astray.
So, seek out the wisdom, that hath been proven right,
And let it guide thy thoughts, both day and night.

And in thy quest for truth, do not be afraid,
To embrace the knowledge, that is still unknown.
For it is in the unknown, that thou shall find,
The greatest discoveries, that shall forever bind.

So, eat of the good, and read of the wise,
For in this way, thou shall grow, both in mind and size.
For thou art what thou eateth, and what thou readeth,
And thus, shall thy spirit, be forever wreathed.

And as thou continue, in thy journey through life,
Never forget, what thou art truly made of.
For thou art the sum, of all that thou hast seen,
And all that thou hast learned, in thy quest for truth within.

And as thou grow, in wisdom and in grace,
Let thy knowledge, be a beacon to all who seek.
For in thy books and in thy food, doth lie the key,
To the secrets of the universe, for all to see.

And though the journey, may be long and hard,
Let not thy spirit, ever falter or be scarred.
For in the end, thou shall stand tall and proud,
And bask in the light, of thy knowledge-endowed.

So, eat well, and read on, with courage in thy heart,
And never forget, what thou art truly made of.
For thou art the essence, of all that is good and right,
And in this way, shall thou find, thy greatest height.

So, let thy knowledge, be a guiding light,
To all who seek the truth, in the world so bright.
And let thy books and thy food, be the keys,
To unlocking the secrets, of the universe and thee.

For thou art what thou eateth and what thou readeth,
And in this truth, shall thou find, thy greatest strength.
And so, may thy journey, be filled with wisdom and grace,
And may thou find, thy greatest truth, in this world of space.

17. Solitude of the Intelligent Mind

Intelligence, a gift bestowed
But with it comes a heavy load
A tendency towards isolation
As we seek our own contemplation

We delve into the deepest depths
Of knowledge and intellect
But in doing so, we may forget
The value of human connection yet

For as we climb the intellectual heights
We risk losing sight
Of those around us, left behind
In the solitude of our own mind

But perhaps it is not intelligence
That drives us to this indifference
But rather a fear of being misunderstood
In a world that values the conventional good

So let us embrace our intellect
But not at the cost of neglect
For in the end, it is connection
That gives life its true affection

18. Flawed Yet Fabulous: Embracing Our Imperfections with Love

When you like yourself, you see your flaws as imperfections,

But when I love you, I see them as unique additions.

I embrace your quirks and your flaws, for they make you who you are,

I love all of you, both near and far.

Take Socrates, for example, with his questioning mind,

His curiosity led him to be one of a kind.

His flaws may have been seen as a problem by some,

But his love for wisdom and truth made him a great one.

Then there's Vincent van Gogh, with his troubled mind and soul,

His paintings may not have been worth much, but they were whole.

His flaws made him who he was, a brilliant artist and man,

His love for his craft was all that he had.

Rosa Parks, with her bravery and strength,

Fought for what she believed in, at any length.

Her flaws may have been seen as a weakness by some,

But her love for justice made her a hero, not a bum.

And let's not forget about Shakespeare, with his pen and wit,

His flaws may have been seen as a burden, but he never quit.

His love for literature and the arts made him a great playwright,
His flaws were just a small part of his light.

So let us love ourselves and others, flaws and all,
For it is in our imperfections that we stand tall.
Embrace your quirks and your flaws, for they make you unique,
And when you love yourself, your confidence will peak.

19. Rising Above: A Journey Beyond Holes

Do not let your goals be spoiled by holes
That undermine and weaken all your efforts.
For when you strive to reach for greater heights,
You must not let your focus be diverted.

For every step along the journey,
There will be obstacles and setbacks,
But if you stay true to your vision,
You will find a way to overcome and surpass it.

So do not let yourself be tempted
By the fleeting joys and pleasures of this world,
For they are but distractions from the task at hand,
And will only lead you down a path unfurled.

Instead, strive for something greater,
Something that will stand the test of time,
And in doing so, you will find a strength
That will help you weather every trial and climb.

For when you are able to rise above
The desires that bind and hold you down,
You will find a freedom and a power
That will help you conquer every obstacle found.

So do not let yourself be swayed
By the fleeting fancies of this life,
But rather focus on the things that truly matter,
And let your goals be free from holes and strife.

20. Beyond Pleasure, Beyond Pain

When a man transcends his craving for pleasure ,
He'll find the strength to bear all sorts of misery.
For pleasure and pain are two sides of the same coin,
And he who masters one, masters the other too.

But to rise above desire is no easy feat,
It requires a strength of will and a noble heart.
For the road to true greatness is often fraught with hardship,
And only those who brave the journey will find their true worth.

So if you wish to be superior to pleasure and pain,
You must first conquer your own desires.
For it is only then that you'll find true peace,
And the power to weather any storm that comes your way.

21. Thoh Tim: A Game of Luck, Dreams, and Culture"

In the city of Shillong, where the hills rise tall
There is a game that captures the hearts of all
The Khasi Hills Archery Sports Association
Organizes a contest, a challenge with passion

Archers from clubs gather at the shooting range
Their aim true, their determination unchanging
Two rounds of archery, each with its own score
Fifty archers shooting thirty, and twenty more

The betting result, it depends on the hits
The number of arrows that land in the pits
A pot to be won, by those who can guess
The last two digits, of the total success

Numbers from zero to ninety-nine are the game
Bets placed low, or high with no shame
For every re. one invested, four thousand could be earned
If both rounds are won, the fire within burned

Two results each day, announced with pride
Displayed on counters, and online aside
Shillong Teer, Khanapara Teer, and Jowai Teer too
This betting extravaganza, a daily affair to pursue

But is it just a game, this betting on chance
Or a reflection of a deeper cultural dance
A desire for success, a yearning for fame
A hope for something more, a life without shame

Perhaps it's a test, a risk we must bear
A chance to prove our worth, to show we can dare
To face the unknown, to embrace the thrill
To live for the moment, to take a chance and chill

But as we bet on luck, and the fates decide
We must also remember, it's not just about pride
It's about community, and the bonds we create
It's about connection, and the love we generate

So let the bets be placed, and the arrows fly
But let us also remember, it's not just about the sky
It's about the journey, the people we meet
It's about the culture, the rhythm of our feet.

Dreams, a realm of the unknown
A realm of the subconscious, where truths are shown
They play a role, in the predictions we make
Of the results of Thoh tim, a game we undertake

For many people, dreams are the way
To place their bets, on a fateful day
They come up with theories, of luck and of fate

Interpreting symbols, to find their right mate

Different ways of interpreting, a code to be cracked
An erotic dream, the number seventeen, packed
Money symbolizes, the number fourteen
A lake, the number six, a dream that's serene

Seeing or getting money, a lucky score
Fourteen, twenty-four, and thirty-four
These are the symbols, the signs we must heed
To place our bets, and fulfill our greed

Number nine for dead, and seven for snake
Different meanings, for each dreamer's sake
They use these theories, to calculate their bet
Hoping their dream, will be their lucky debt

But is it just a game, this betting on dreams
Or a reflection of something deeper it seems
Perhaps it's a connection, to a world unseen
A way to tap into, a power supreme

Dreams have a meaning, a message to impart
A way to explore, the depths of the heart
A chance to learn, and grow from within
A way to find peace, and let go of sin

So let the bets be placed, on the strength of a dream
But let us also remember, it's not just about the scheme

It's about the journey, the growth we can find
It's about the connection, to the powers of the mind

For dreams are more than just a fleeting night
They are a guide, a beacon of light
They offer wisdom, and understanding too
A way to tap into, the world we knew.

But it's not just about luck, and the numbers we choose
It's about the philosophy, the culture we muse
For dreams are more than just a passing fancy
They're a reflection of the soul, a divine chancy

They offer insight, a glimpse of the future
A chance to explore, the possibilities to nurture
So as we bet on Thoh tim, and the numbers we play
Let us also remember, it's not just about the fray

Thoh Tim, a game of chance and skill
A contest of archers, a thrill to fulfill
In the city of Shillong, where the hills rise tall
There is a betting extravaganza, a game for all

But alas, there is a line that must be drawn
For the addictive nature of betting, can't be ignored
Employees at the archery counter, they take a stand
Prohibiting the young, from joining in hand

For Thoh Tim can be a dangerous game

A lure of quick riches, a way to tame
The restless spirit, the hungry soul
But at what cost, the toll

For betting can be a slippery slope
Leading to addiction, a never-ending hope
Of hitting the jackpot, of changing one's fate
But at what price, the weight

It's about the dreams, the messages they bring
It's about the culture, the traditions they sing
It's about the community, the bonds we create
It's about the connection, and the love we generate.

The game of betting, it holds great allure
A chance at riches, a path to mature
But there is a darkness, a shadow that lurks
A side that can't be ignored, a side that can irk

For gambling, it can be a vicious cycle
A never-ending spiral, a path that is volatile
It becomes badly addictive, when we lose more than we earn
A pattern that repeats, a cycle that never turns

Psychiatrists compare it to alcohol's effect
A lure that can trap, a force to deflect
Many gamblers, they come from weak economic grounds
Investing a significant sum, with quick profits abound

But such profits are never guaranteed
In the nature of the sport, they are not deemed
To be a possibility, a chance to be had
Leaving many gamblers, feeling sad

In the past, issues have arisen, a consequence of the game
Domestic violence, debt burdens, and petty crime to name
A few of the problems, that have cropped up due to addiction
A vicious cycle, a force to resist with conviction

So let us be cautious, as we place our bets
Remembering the risks, and the debts
That can come with the thrill, the rush of the game
But let us also remember, it's not just about the fame

For betting is more than just a game
It's a philosophy, a cultural claim
To the power of the mind, the control of the hand
To the unity of body, and the strength of the band

So let the arrows fly, and the targets be met
But let us also remember, it's not just about the bet
It's about the culture, the traditions we keep
It's about the community, the friendships we reap.

22. Etched in Memory: A Sonnet of Regret and Desolation

Per diem, I asperate to attain a tenure

Of augmented opulence, yet I cannot neglect

Those sauté moments that I am incessantly

Preoccupied with in my epochs of tribulation

And antecedent transgression which I had done

To traverse through my time and space of my existence.

They incessantly agitate me quotidianly,

Destroying each and every juncture of my moments

Of felicity. The past, an ever-present weight

That bears upon my mind, my heart, my soul,

A constant source of lamentation and regret

That leaves me in a state of desolation

And dejection, unable to forget

The errors of my ways, the deeds of my transgression.

But I must strive to transcend this burden of the past,

And learn to let go of my regrets and guilt,

For dwelling on the past, will forever last.

I must learn to forgive myself, and move on,

For only in forgiveness, can true healing begin,

And true growth and redemption can be won.

For the past is but a fleeting moment in time,
And it's not worth sacrificing our present and future,
For the sake of dwelling on past mistakes and crimes.

So let us strive to learn from our past,
And use it as a tool for growth and self-improvement,
And not let it define and hold us back.

For true strength lies in our ability to forgive,
And to let go of the past, and move forward with grace,
And in so doing, find true peace and serenity.

And as we journey through life, let us not forget
The importance of self-reflection and introspection,
For it is in understanding ourselves, that we truly connect.

Let us take the time to delve deep within,
To explore our thoughts, emotions and desires,
For it is through this self-exploration that true growth begins.

And in this growth, we find true strength and fortitude,
For it allows us to navigate life's twists and turns with grace,
And to rise above our own limitations, with gratitude.

Let us strive to live in the present moment,
And not let the past or the future consume us,
For it is in the present that true happiness is found.

Let us embrace the beauty and uncertainty of life,
And not fear change or the unknown,
For it is through these challenges that we truly thrive.

So let us strive to overcome our past transgression,
And find inner peace and redemption,
Through self-forgiveness and self-transcendence.

And in so doing, let us find true strength and solace,
As we journey through this mortal reality,
With humility, and a heart full of purpose.

23. Children of nobody

They may be labeled as outcasts, but they hold a special grace,
Their resilience and determination, a sight to behold in this place.

They may have been dealt a tough hand, but they'll play it with all their might,
They'll climb every obstacle, and reach for the stars that shine so bright.

Their journey may be difficult, but they'll never falter or sway,
For they know that they deserve to live, and have the right to pave their own way.

So let us not judge them, for their struggles are not of their own making,
Let us lend them a helping hand, for the children of nobody are worth saving.

24. Melancholy of Ka tangmuri

In this realm of enigma and desuetude,
Where beauty and tradition are but fleeting illusions,
The melifluous vibrations of Ka tangmuri are now subdued,
A victim of the ceaseless march of time's dilutions.

Gone are the aeons of cultural grandiosity,
Replaced by a world of emptiness and superficiality.
Where history is ignored, and the present is lugubrious,
The melifluous vibrations of Ka tangmuri can no longer be heard with clarity.

For the world is consumed by its own base desires,
And the aesthetic appeal of culture is now but a mirage.
We are lost in the enigma of our own making,
And the melifluous vibrations of Ka tangmuri are now but a forgotten storage.

Thus, let us lament the loss of our historical legacy,
And the aesthetic appeal of culture that could never endure,
For in this realm of enigma and desuetude,
The melifluous vibrations of Ka tangmuri can no longer be diffused,
A reflection of the human condition, fleeting, futile and obscure.

25. Transience and Camaraderie: A Chance Encounter at the Lake

Effulgence is a transient phenomenon,
A delicate blossom that flourishes and wanes.
Like the vernal blossoms of spring,
Its radiance swiftly descends.

It's a transient emotion, like the breeze,
A juncture of delight that transpires in a trice.
As transient as the felicity that Alice discovers,
When she plummets down the burrow, in a race.

Effulgence is a transient phenomenon,
A sensation that arises and dissipates.
Like the cheer that Holden uncovers,
When he discovers his sister, Phoebe, in Central Park, I surmise.

But though effulgence may be transient,
It's worth the pursuit, and worth the wait.
For even though it may not abide,
Its radiance and delight can still resonate.

But as I stand here, on the chill iron balustrades of the lake of the
university,

I can't help but ponder about the world around me.
Those fish, they leap and frolic,
So carefree and joyful, relishing the popcorn I threw.
The twenty geese come to partake in the feast,
Their honks and quacks filling the air.

But as I observe these creatures, I am reminded of a phrase
From the great bard, William Shakespeare:
"We are such stuff as dreams are made on."
Like the fish, we too are transient and ephemeral,
Our time on this earth but a fleeting instant in the grand scheme.

And yet, I see the children next to me,
Shouting and screaming with glee,
So full of life and vitality,
Unaware of the transient nature of their own being.

But perhaps that is the beauty of it all,
This ignorance of our own mortality.
It allows us to live fully,
To embrace each moment as it comes,
To laugh and love and experience all the world has to offer.

So I stand here, on the chill iron balustrades of the lake,
Observing the world around me,
Finding delight in the simple pleasures of life,
Embracing the present moment,
And living fully, just like those fish.

I see the beauty in this simple act,
A moment of pure and unbridled joy.
It reminds me of a line from Keats,
"The poetry of earth is never dead."

For in this moment, I am alive,
I am present and content.
This, my friends, is true effulgence,
A state of mind, not just a sensation.

Let us all find our own effulgence,
In the smallest of moments, the most mundane of days.
For it is there, in the ordinary,
That we find the extraordinary.

Effulgence is a transient moment,
A chance encounter with a dear old friend.
Kali Chand greets me with cheer,
Uncle Atul with blessings that never end.

Suddenly, a tap on the back that makes me turn
Brings me face to face with Anna Sachin Anand
We shake hands and greet each other,
By the lake of NEHU, our meeting unplanned

Like the chance encounter of the knight and squire
In Don Quixote, or the chance meeting of Romeo and Juliet
Our meeting was not predetermined, but rather left to chance

Yet, perhaps it was not chance at all
But rather the hand of fate, guiding us together
Like the puppets in Oedipus controlled by the gods
If that is what they believed.

Perchance, it was the decisions we had made
The itinerary we had chosen, that led us to this juncture
Like the crossroads in Homer's epic, where one choice leads to fate

Be that as it may, our congregation here today
Is a reminder of the might of the capricious
The allure of the unknown, that lies just beyond the bend.

Myself and Anna Sachin Anand,
Two confidants, reunited after a hiatus.
Our camaraderie as robust as ever,
A luminescent beacon that never wanes.

We chortled and cherished our fortuitous rendezvous,
A chance encounter that brought us felicity.
Nine minutes we spent together,
But it felt like an aeon.

Six years have transpired since we last met,
During our collegiate days and student life.
But time has not dulled our camaraderie,
It remains a constant, shining brilliant.

Like the friendship between Frodo and Sam,

In J.R.R. Tolkien's The Lord of the Rings.
Their camaraderie forged in the fires of adversity,
A camaraderie that carried them through their odyssey.

Or the enduring friendship between Sherlock and Watson,
In Arthur Conan Doyle's tales of enigma.
Their camaraderie unbreakable, even in the face of danger,
A friendship that stands the test of time.

Myself and Anna Sachin Anand ,
Two confidants, bound together by a camaraderie that never wanes.
A luminescent beacon in a dark and uncertain world,
A friendship to be cherished and forever celebrated.

Euphoria is found in the little things,
The unexpected moments that bring us joy.
It's the love and blessings of those we hold dear,
That bring euphoria and fill us with pride.

Old friends are like a chrono machine,
Transporting us back to our youth,
To the days of carefree laughter,
When we were just starting out.

We recall the memories we made,
The late nights studying and discoursing ,
The adventures and misadventures,
The friendships that will always stay.

Like Holden Caulfield and Phoebe,
We laughed and loved and learned,
We shared our hopes and fears,
And discovered who we were.

Like Elizabeth Bennet and Mr. Darcy,
We crossed paths and sparked a flame,
We challenged and inspired each other,
And grew together all the same.

Old friends are a treasure,
A reminder of who we once were,
And who we will always be,
Bonded by memories that endure.

Six years ago, I stood with Anna Sachin Anand
In protest at our university hostel
But after graduation, he returned home
We took our own road and back home.

I told him of the worker's protest I now lead
At NEHU, where we've sat days and night for ninety days
Occupying the entrance to the Vice Chancellor's office
Demanding change in the way we're treated, a voice

Anna Sachin Anand was excited to hear
Of the progress we'd made, but also a bit regretful
That he couldn't be there with me, standing strong
In solidarity, fighting for what's right and wrong

Anna Sachin Anand, my dearest amicus,
Was thrilled to hear of the advancements we'd made,
But also tinged with a hint of regret
That he could not stand by my side, in support

For, as Jean-Paul Sartre so astutely stated,
"Freedom is what we do with what is done to us."
And like the protagonists in George Orwell's "1984,"
We must resist the forces that seek to control us
And fight for our freedom, at any cost

So I shall continue the battle, with Anna Sachin Anand in my heart,
For justice, equality, and the right to a better beginning
In this world that can be brutal and unjust,
But where we possess the power to make a difference, if we dare

For a mere nine minutes, I conversed with my old friend,
But as the wise old Bard wrote in his sonnets, time is fleeting,
And though we desired a longer conversation,
Anna Sachin Anand had to depart, back to Guwahati, seventy
kilometres away

But in that brief moment of connection,
We discovered something more profound than mere affection,
Like Anna Sachin Anand in "Birdsong,"
We found a bond that was unbreakable

A treasure more valuable than gold,

A glimpse of friendship that will never grow old,
Like the bond between Bilbo and Frodo in "The Lord of the Rings,"
A friendship that rings true and eternal

A memory to treasure forever,
A bond that we'll hold dear, no matter the weather,
Like the bond between Sherlock and Watson in "Sherlock Holmes,"
A friendship that no force can shatter, no matter how grim the circumstances

We feel that kind of brotherhood in our blood and bones,
A bond that we'll always hold close,
A bond that will never be overthrown,
For in that brief moment of connection,
We found a treasure more valuable than gold,
A glimpse of friendship's enduring bond,
A memory to treasure forever

Like Proust's madeleine,
This moment will stay with me,
A reminder of the significance of human connection,
A reminder to savor every precious moment

So let us embrace the fleeting nature of life,
And seize every opportunity to connect,
For in the end, it is not the long conversations,
But the brief, precious moments that truly matter

As I stand here, watching my old friend depart,

I am reminded of the poem by Emily Dickinson, "Parting is all we know of heaven, and all we need of hell."
For in this moment, as Anna Sachin Anand leaves me,
I feel the pain of separation, the weight of loss

But as I reflect on our time together, on the memories we have made,
I am reminded of the words of Ralph Waldo Emerson, "The only way to have a friend is to be one."
Anna Sachin Anand has been a true friend to me,
A man of great wit and charm, always ready with a joke or a clever remark

So as he leaves, I cannot help but feel a heavy heart,
But I also know that our friendship will endure, even across the miles,
For as Shakespeare wrote in Romeo and Juliet, "Distance cannot hinder, nor time defeat true friendship."
Our bond is strong, and I know that our paths will cross again

As I bid adieu to my dear and cherished companion,
Anna Sachin Anand, my bosom friend,
My heart is heavy with sorrow, yet filled with optimism,
For though he departs to his native land in Kerela,
His essence shall forever reside within my being.

My mind wanders back to the moments we shared,
The nocturnal discussions of love and existence,
The moments of mirth and sorrow we bore,
And I am eternally grateful for the duration of our companionship.

But as I bid farewell, I am reminded of Proust's musings,
That true paradise is that which is lost,
And as we bid farewell, I am left with a sense of loss,
But also with a glimmer of hope, that our paths shall cross.

Anna Sachin Anand, my dear and cherished companion,
I bid thee farewell, but know that our bond shall never truly end,
For as Rilke so eloquently stated,
Friendship is a high art, one that requires devotion and care,
And that is exactly what we have shared, a friendship that shall always
be there.

As you embark on your new journey,
Like Odysseus in Homer's epic tale,
In search of self-discovery and your true home,
And like Frodo in the Lord of the Rings,
May you face challenges and obstacles,
But with determination and valor,
Emerge victorious.

As I return to Nehu lake,
To tend to the avian and aquatic life,
I shall always remember our friendship,
And the memories we shared.

Farewell, Anna Sachin Anand,
My dear and cherished companion,
May our paths cross again in the future,
As we continue on our journey through life.

As I sit by the waters, contemplating my existence,
Confronting my own absurdity and the Sisyphean task of life,
I am comforted by Thoreau's words,
That the mass of men lead lives of quiet desperation,
But I choose to live, to find my own path,
To tend to the avian and aquatic life,
And to find my own purpose and meaning,
Like the journey of the pilgrim,
In search of inner peace.

So I choose to keep on living,
To find my own way, my own truth,
To tend to the avian and aquatic life,
And to lay down my boulder, when my time is due,
For in this world, there is more than just survival,
There is love and hope, and the chance to thrive.

26. Hiraeth for Childhood Days

A time when life was simple and free
The days of childhood, full of joy and cheer
When our mother went to market, we'd wait eagerly

For she'd bring us treats, a chicken chow or momo
Wrapped in Phrynium pubinerve leaves, the scent a memory still
A moment frozen in time, a Smultronställe
When all our troubles seemed so far and chill

But hiraeth, it lingers in our hearts
A longing for the past that's now long gone
A time when life was full of little parts
That made it sweet and bright and full of song

So let us cherish hiraeth, this yearning
For the memories that keep our hearts burning.

27. Summoned by Fate: A Call to Action

In verbiage void of utility,
Let us not squander precious hours.
For opportunity doth now proffer,
A chance for us to exert our powers.

Not every day doth fate summon forth,
A call to make our worth manifest.
Let us then seize this moment of worth,
Ere it be lost to time's behest.

With purposeful gait and hearts aglow with ambition,
We shall engender change, ignite the spark.
Though beset with obstacles, we'll persevere,
And earn a legacy that shall outlast the dark.

Therefore, let us abstain from idle prate,
And rise to action ere our chance abate.

28. The Misfortune of the Five Hundred Rupees: A Cautionary Tale

Upon my journey in a maxi-cab, I encountered a sot,

Who persisted in inquiring about my apparel, like a pastor,

He confided in me of his past as a bodyguard of a parish priest,

And spoke of his acrimonious existence, preferring whiskey over water,

And tobacco rolls in place of sustenance.

But even in his drunken state, he maintained a semblance of self-preservation,

Eating vegetables for vitamins, and meats for protein.

But as he rambled on about the 2023 General Election,

I couldn't help but perceive the tragedy,

Of a man who had been bought for a mere five hundred rupees and a bottle of whiskey,

To cast his vote for a friend contesting in the impending month.

All of which serves as a cautionary tale of the perils of the pursuit of power and fame,

And the bitter consequences that inevitably accompany such endeavors.

29. Whispers in the Night: The Duality of Dreams and Thoh Tim (Teer)

Dreams are like a fleeting breeze,
A whisper in the night,
A bridge between the waking world
And the realm of shadows bright.

In many stories, dreams are revered,
As a source of wisdom and insight,
A path to understanding and growth,
A guiding light.

Like the tale of the Bamboo Cutter,
Who dreamt of a child of the moon,
Whose beauty and kindness surpassed all,
And whose love he would pursue.

Or the legend of the fox spirit,
Who dreamed of a prince in disguise,
Whose true form was revealed in sleep,
And whose love he would prize.

Dreams are a canvas of the soul,
A tapestry of our deepest desires,

A reflection of who we are,
And who we aspire to be.

Sometimes they are simple and mundane,
A reflection of our daily lives,
Other times they are bizarre and absurd,
A jumble of nonsensical rhymes.

But it is in these strange and twisted dreams,
That we find the seeds of inspiration,
For it is in the darkest corners of our minds,
That the brightest ideas are born.

So let us embrace our dreams,
No matter how strange or silly they may seem,
For they are the fuel that fires our creativity,
And the driving force behind our ambitions.

And who knows, perhaps in our wildest dreams,
We will find the key to unlock our potential,
And the courage to pursue our dreams,
With all the strength and determination,
That the Khasi tribe displays in their traditional sport of Thoh Tim or
archery betting.

Thoh Tim or Teer, a sport of Meghalaya,
A unique blend of archery and betting,
Governed by law, and yet, so controversial,
A source of both pride and condemnation.

Some see it as a tradition, a way of life,
A test of skill and strength, a rite of passage,
A celebration of culture and community,
A source of entertainment and enjoyment.

Others view it as a vice, a form of gambling,
A temptation to be avoided, a source of corruption,
A threat to the moral fabric of society,
A drain on the resources of the state.

But what is the true nature
of Thoh Tim or Teer?
Is it a sport or a sin?
A tradition or a temptation?
A blessing or a curse?
A source of pride or shame?

the game of Thoh Tim or Teer,
Involved archers from different clubs,
Gathering at a shooting range to test their skills,
To see who could shoot the most arrows on target.

It was a celebration of culture and tradition,
A way for the people of Meghalaya,
To come together and share in the joys of archery,
And to honor the ancient art of bow and arrow.

As the years went by, and the world transformed

Thoh Tim, or Teer, it's popularity stormed
And with it, the potential for income arose
A source of revenue for the government chose

But for shop owners, a different tale is told
Of exploitation and manipulation, a story uncontrolled
Where workers are underpaid, and left to their fate
While the dreamers busy calculate, in hopes of their fate

For Thoh Tim, it's a game of chance
A gamble on luck, a dance with circumstance
But for some, it's a way of life
A source of income, a chance to strive

But let us not forget, the cost that it bears
The exploitation, the manipulation, the debts and the fears
For as we play this game, we must remember to care
For our community, and the bonds we share.

Some saw this Thoh Tim as a positive development,
A way to modernize and monetize,
A traditional sport, and to bring it into the mainstream,
A source of pride and prosperity for all.

Others viewed it with skepticism,
As a threat to the integrity of the game,
A temptation to corruption and greed,
A violation of the spirit of the sport.

But what is the true meaning of Thoh Tim or Teer?
Is it a source of revenue or a source of conflict?
A celebration of culture or a commercialization of tradition?
A source of pride or a source of shame?

Perhaps it is all these things, and more,
A reflection of the complexities of human nature,
A reminder of the duality of life,
The light and the dark, the good and the bad,
The joy and the sorrow, the hope and the fear.

In the city of Shillong, where the hills rise tall
There are counters on every corner, where bets are placed small
Numbers on boards, a gamble to take
A chance at riches, or a heartache to make

Fortune favors the bold, they say
Those who take risks and make their play
In the world of gambling, where luck is key
Some earn their riches, while others may flee

There are tales of gamblers, in literature and song
Who wagered it all, and yet still came out strong
Take the gentleman gambler, in "The Gambler" by Fyodor Dostoevsky
He played the game with skill, and won great luxury

Or the dashing James Bond, in Ian Fleming's "Casino Royale"
He played the game with finesse, and emerged the victor, employed
These stories show us that fortune may come to those who dare

To take a risk, and play the game with skill and care

As the cards are dealt and the dice are thrown,
The fortunes of men are forever known.
Some take betting and gambling with great care,
But others fall prey to the siren's snare.

Fortune's fickle game, the risk of winning or losing,
Ahead of all your plans, a test of your choosing.
You bet on your luck, your skill, your judgment,
Hoping for a reward, a prize, a settlement.

From Shakespeare's tragic King Lear,
We see a man who lost all he held dear.
He gave away his kingdom and wealth,
Trusting in the false love of his children, in stealth.

In F. Scott Fitzgerald's The Great Gatsby,
We see a man who gambles on love, but ends up losing his way.
Jay Gatsby's obsession with Daisy leads to his downfall,
Leaving him penniless and alone, standing tall.

Shakespeare's Othello,
Bet on the wrong horse,
Trusting in the deceitful Iago,
Leaving him penniless and divorced.

Or the story of the merchant Shylock
Who gambled with his very soul

He lost all his wealth, his honor, and his dock
And was left with nothing, a mere fool

In "The Gambler," Fyodor Dostoevsky
Chronicles the tale of a man so risky
He bet his life, and lost it all
His fortunes gone, his fate so small

There's Midas, the king who craved gold,
But lost his daughter, his touch, his soul.
There's Gatsby, the tycoon who dreamed of fame,
But paid with his life, his love, his name.

There's Fortunato, the fool who mocked the jester,
But met his death in the vaults, the poison, the terror.
There's Alekhine, the chess grandmaster who played for power,
But fell to his own devices, his rivals, his hour.

In "Of Mice and Men," George and Lennie
Dreamed of owning their own land.
They bet on their friendship and their strength,
But fate had other plans in hand.

But the dream, it seems, is also fickle,
A mirage that vanishes in the light.
As Holden Caulfield learns in "The Catcher in the Rye,"
Sometimes the dream is just an endless, endless fight.

The Pied Piper of Hamelin,

Promising to lead the rats away,
But only if the town would pay,
A risk they were willing to take.

Even the Tortoise and the Hare,
A bet on who would win the race,
A chance to achieve their dreams,
A dream worth chasing with grace.

From tales of childhood, we learned of this dream
A golden goose, a beanstalk, a genie's gleam
A pot of gold at the end of a rainbow's arc
A magic carpet, a mermaid's song, a phoenix's spark

Like Jack who climbed the beanstalk
Or Alice who fell down the rabbit hole
We dream of adventure and wonder
And the chance to be something more

As in "The Alchemist," we see a different kind of dream,
One that is not so easily won. Santiago seeks his personal legend,
A journey that requires much more than simple luck.

We see it in the words of Martin Luther King
"I have a dream" he did sing
A dream of equality, justice, and peace
A dream we all long for, without cease

And in the tales of Don Quixote, we see

A man who dreamed of chivalry
He chased his dream, with heart ablaze
A hero in his own, unique way

The dream, it's a driving force, a guiding star
We chase it, in hopes it won't be far
For in our dreams, we find our hope
A chance to reach for the stars, to cope

what is it that drives us to take such risks?
Is it the allure of wealth and success?
Or is it a deeper, more philosophical quest
For the elusive concept of "luck"?

Is Thoh Tim merely a game, a mere bet on fate
Or a cultural expression, a dance to elate
A desire for achievement, a hunger for fame
A hope for transcendence, a life free of blame

Thoh tim , a test of our courage and soul
A chance to prove ourselves, to be whole
To face the unknown, to embrace the thrill
To live in the moment, to take a chance and chill

In the midst of this cultural rite
We seek to prove our worth, to ignite
The fire within us, to live and be true
To embrace the risk, to see it through

But as we bet on luck, and the fates decide
We must also remember, it's not just about pride
It's about community, and the bonds we create
It's about connection, and the love we generate

30. Rhapsody of 'Ka tangmuri'

Ka tangmuri, a masterpiece of design,
With its conical bore and delicate wooden frame,
Boasts a mouthpiece, reed, and fingerholes,
A melodious source, that forever remains.

A narrow grass reed, broad at one end,
Inserted into the mouthpiece, in perfect blend,
Secured by a slender metal staple,
Its high-pitched tones, never fail.

An emblem of culture, and ancient traditions,
Ka tangmuri's sound, an untold edition.
A connection to the past and present,
A source of delight, that forever presents.

Ka tangmuri's sound,
A simple instrument, yet profound.
Reminding us of our cultural heritage,
And the beauty of music, that always concurs.

The queen of instruments, Ka tangmuri,
A symbol of culture, and traditions that are free,
Widely performed in the Meghalaya region,

Bringing joy and light to every season.

With seven holes on its tube,
Ka tangmuri's sound, never dull and crude.
Associated with the dance, Ka Shad Nong Krem,
A religious ritual, that is always gem.

A tradition among the Khasi and Jaintia of hills,
And neighboring regions, Ka tangmuri still fills,
A part of traditional rituals and songs,
Connecting us to our roots, forever long.

Let us celebrate the Ka tangmuri's sound,
An emblem of culture, that is always bound,
To the traditions of the past and present,
A source of joy, that forever presents.

31. The Ikigai Journey

Ikigai, a reason to be
A sense of purpose, a source of glee
It's that thing that drives us forward
The reason we wake up each day

It's the passion that fills our hearts
The joy that sets our souls ablaze
It's the reason we give it our all
And the motivation to face each challenge that comes our way

Ikigai, a source of strength
A guiding light through the darkest of days
It gives us hope and helps us persevere
Through the struggles and the pains

It's the balance between work and play
The harmony of body, mind and soul
It's the path to true contentment
And the secret to feeling whole

Ikigai, a gift from within
A wellspring of happiness and bliss
It's the spark that ignites our spirit
And guides us on a journey of endless possibility

32. Soothing Reflections: My Anaesthetic Voice

My anaesthetic voice, a foggy haze,
A distant sound, beyond the light of day.
I drift and dream, my body numb and still,
As the surgeons work, their hands with skill.

But even as I lay unconscious here,
My voice, it speaks, a quiet, distant cheer.
It whispers softly, a gentle soothing tone,
As I journey through this surgery alone.

For even when my body's weak and frail,
My voice remains, a steady, guiding trail.
It leads me through the darkness and the pain,
Until I wake, and the world comes back again.

So let my anaesthetic voice be heard,
A gentle guide, through all that's absurd.
For even when I'm lost in deepest sleep,
It whispers on, a soothing, endless keep.

33. The Big Brother's Reign: A 1984 Perspective

Big Brother looms large
In our society of 1984
Watching our every move
With telescreens and more

Thoughtcrime is a sin
In this world of control
To have rebellious thoughts
Is to risk your very soul

Newspeak is the language
Of this world we're in
Designed to limit thought
And keep us all within

Doublethink is required
To survive and thrive
Simultaneously accepting
Contradictory lies

The memory hole devours
All that is not deemed right
Erasing history's wrongs
From our memory's sight

The Proles, the working class
Are not watched with such care
They are left to their own devices
In this world unfair

The Ministry of Truth
Spins its web of deceit
Propaganda and revisionism
Our minds it does cheat

The Ministry of Love
Tortures and brainwashes
Erasing all dissent
In this society rash

The Ministry of Peace
Wages endless war
Fueled by hate and fear
Forever wanting more

The Ministry of Plenty
Controls our every bite
Rationing our resources
In this world of might

We are trapped, oppressed
By this society's hold
Our lives controlled

By Big Brother's scold

34. Cheddar , My Love's Favourite

A feline grace, so elegant and nimble
A sylvan beauty, wild and enigmatic
Poised and fastidious, a true plush queen
Lithe and coquettish, a sight unseen

But there is more to this fabled feline
Than beauty and grace, so felicitous and fine
For she holds within her a feral heart
Wild and free, never forced to part

With sinuous movements, she prowls the land
Majestic and ethereal, a true Sylvan grand
Her coat pristine, svelte and sleek
A dapper creature, truly unique

But do not be fooled by her nonchalant air
For she is agile, and ever aware
Elongated and efficacious, she stalks her prey
A force to be reckoned with, come what may

Cheddar a fabled feline form
Ethereal and majestic, a true sylvan norm
Agile and graceful, a sight to behold
A true masterpiece, never growing old.

35. The Fate of Huckleberry Finn

The fate of Huckleberry Finn
Is one of adventure and strife
On a journey down the river
He learned about life

With his friend Tom Sawyer
He ran from society's norms
Searching for freedom
On the Mississippi's banks to form

But as he traveled downstream
He was faced with moral dilemmas galore
Should he turn in the runaway slave
Or stand up for what he was fighting for

In the end, Huck chose his conscience
Over the expectations of the world
He helped Jim to freedom
And his own flag unfurled

The fate of Huckleberry Finn
Is a tale of growth and change
From a reckless boy to a man
Who found his own way, who rearranged

Society's rules and restrictions
In favor of what he knew to be right
Huck Finn's journey teaches us
To stand up for what we believe, to fight

For what we know to be just
Even if it goes against the grain
For in the end, it is our own fate
That we must choose, that we must sustain

36. Ode to The Spirit of Parrot

A parrot's spirit knows no bounds
Its energy and playfulness astounds
It hops and flits from branch to branch
A blur of color, a joyful splash

Its wings a blur as it takes to flight
Soaring through the air with all its might
A creature free, with wild abandon
Embracing life, with joy and candor

But as I watch this feathered friend
I can't help but think, does it comprehend
The vast expanse of all the world
The mysteries and secrets yet unfurled

For even in its playful flight
There lies a depth of meaning and insight
A reminder to embrace each day
To live and love in our own unique way

37. The Melancholy of Ka Tangmuri: A Lament for Lost Culture.

Ah, alas! In this realm of obscurity and desolation,
The melodious strains of Ka tangmuri can no longer be disseminated.
For the traditions of yore, are rapidly becoming anachronistic,
And with them, the aesthetic splendor of Ka tangmuri's performance.

Gone are the eras of cultural grandiosity,
Replacement with a world that is superficial and extensive.
Where the annals are disregarded, and the current state is dreary,
The melodious strains of Ka tangmuri can no longer convey.

For the world is saturated with avarice and ambition,
And the aesthetic appeal of culture is no longer in question.
We are lost in the obscurity of our own creation,
And the melodious strains of Ka tangmuri are no longer forsaken.

Thus, let us bemoan the loss of our historical legacy,
And the aesthetic appeal of culture that could never endure.
For in this realm of obscurity and desolation,
The melodious strains of Ka tangmuri can no longer be disseminated.

By Mawphniang Napoleon

38. Timeless Love in Vellore

The first time I beheld you,
You were a curious young woman,
Whose name, Kongduh Khyriemujat, I learned was from Nongkrem,
Though your baptismal appellation remains unknown to me,
My timidity preventing me from inquiring.

We both found ourselves hospitalized at the esteemed Christian
Medical College in Vellore,
You there for your uncle, who suffered from laryngeal cancer,
While I was there for my cousin, who was afflicted with gastric ulcers.

Due to the abundance of patients, we were obliged to sleep on the
streets,
The first day we conversed, I was flustered and too reticent to ask about
your lineage.
But at the same time, I was proud and delighted to meet a Khasi lady
such as yourself, so far from my village.
You were fluent in the Khasi language, while I am proficient in my
Bhoi dialect.
I remember you were reading "The Alchemist,"
And I was merely holding a Dumakyllain, my tobacco roll purchased
in Nongstoin.
Your smile made me happier and gave me a sense of maternal love.
Gradually, we became friends and learned more about each other.
We stayed at the hospital for 131 days, until love flourished between

us.

A strong connection, a love that fully bloomed.

You, sweet and intelligent, me, just a rustic youth,
You, attending school in Thiruvananthapuram for a decade, far from home,
Living in a hostel, me just a small town lad,
But together, we enjoyed numerous cups of tea, chocolate, and late night adventures, like urbanites.

But abruptly, it all came to an end,
Your uncle passed away, forcing you to return home and attend to your duties.
I was heartbroken, we had no means of communication.
Too young to comprehend love, too young to cope with the emotions.

Kongduh, my heart was shattered when you left,
But the memories remain, forever etched in my mind.
Though we may never meet again, never lay eyes on each other,
My love for you, Kongduh, will always persist.

Intangible, yet ever-present,
This love that was born in a hospital bed,
A love that defies space and time,
A love that will always be intertwined.

But alas, life goes on, and we must as well,
Moving forward, with memories of what we once had.
Yet the love we shared will never fade,

A timeless bond, a love that was meant to be.

For even though we may be separated by miles and years,
Our love will always be with us, it never fades.
It will stay with us, a beacon of hope and light,
A reminder of the love we shared, a love that was true and right.

So here's to you, Kongduh, my love, my friend,
May our love continue to transcend
All barriers and boundaries, all doubts and fears,
And may it remain a constant, a love that is clear and pure.

39. Cruel Jest: A Journey Through Life

Life, a cruel joke played upon us all
A never-ending cycle, a never-ending fall
We are born into this world, innocent and pure
But soon we learn, the truth, the cure

For life is filled with pain, with suffering and strife
We struggle through, trying to find a way to life
We face hardship, we face adversity
We are battered, we are beaten, we are tested, endlessly

We search for meaning, for purpose, for a reason to be
But the more we search, the more we see
That life is a riddle, a puzzle, a game
A test of our mettle, a test of our aim

We try to make sense, of this world that we live in
But the more we try, the more we spin
In circles, in cycles, a never-ending reel
A game that we play, a game that we feel

So what is the point, of this life that we lead
A constant struggle, a constant need
To make sense, to find purpose, to find our way
But in the end, it all fades away

Life is a journey, a road that we take
But in the end, it's a journey we forsake
For in the end, we return to dust
A cycle of life, a cycle of lust

So let us embrace, the beauty of the journey
The pain, the struggle, the joy and the misery
For in the end, it is all that we have
Life, a pessimistic epic, a story to be told

40. the Nurse with a Heart of Gold

Oh Kongmem, the nurse of civil hospital Shillong
Whose soft hands bring comfort with the injection's song
Hailing from Bhoi, a woman of kind
With a love and sweetness that is hard to find

When I was admitted with my gall bladder stones
You were there, a light in the hospital's unknowns
Your gentle touch, your soothing words
A balm to my pain, a flight of the birds

I felt a crush, a heart that was broken
As I left the hospital, my heart unspoken
For I am but a poor boy, without a phone
To ask for your number, to be left alone

But alas, I knew it could not be
For Kongmem, you were already married, a love that was free
So I must accept my heart's desire
And bid farewell to my hospital's choir

But still, I am grateful for the time we had
A memory to cherish, a love that was sad
For Kongmem, you will always be
A sweet nurse, a kind memory

41. Frosty Dawn in Shillong

I wake up from my thirty minute nap
Feeling groggy, sleepy, a little bit horny, perhaps
I check my smartwatch, tracking my sleep patterns of the night
Only two minutes of deep sleep, such a sorry sight

I venture outside, greeted by the morning light
The frosty air of Shillong, a frigid delight
The sunlight filters through the leaves, a green array
The morning dew is sucked up by the sun's warm ray

The dogs are running, playing in the sunshine's glow
A joyous sight, a beauty to behold
I am struck by the beauty of the nature around
The frost, the sun, the dogs on the ground

It fills me with a sense of peace and love
A reminder of the beauty, of the things above
The world may be a troubled place, filled with strife
But moments like these bring solace to my life

42. Ode to the Room Heater

The room heater, a simple machine
But oh, how it warms our hearts and screens
A beacon of heat in the cold, dark night
Bringing comfort and peace, a delight

But is it just a mere object, a tool
Or does it hold deeper meaning, a jewel
Perhaps it represents the warmth of love
The love we give, the love we receive, above

Or maybe it symbolizes the flame of hope
That burns within us, a way to cope
With the trials and tribulations of life
The room heater, a source of light

But as we sit in its warm embrace
We must also consider its place
In the larger scheme of things, its impact
On the earth and its natural pact

For every source of heat, there is a cost
A burden on the environment, a loss
So as we revel in its warmth and cheer
We must also consider its impact, clear

The room heater, a humble yet powerful force
Bringing comfort and joy to all, of course
But let us not forget its place and cost
And strive to use it wisely, without loss.

43. In Search of Certainty: The Paradox of Life and Belief

The paradox of life, an agnostic's plight
To seek and search, but never quite
I am unsure of what lies beyond
Is there a God, or is it all just a task?
I do not believe in a higher power or deity,
But I cannot deny the mysteries of life's clarity.

I do not believe in a higher power or deity,
But I cannot deny the mysteries of life's clarity.

I am an agnostic, a soul in search
Of truth and meaning in this world so vast
But as I ponder and reflect on life
I find myself caught in a paradox rife

On one hand, I crave for certainty
A firm foundation to stand and be
But on the other, I am drawn to doubt
Uncertain of what it is life is about

It seems that every answer I find
Brings with it more questions intertwined

Like a snake eating its own tail
This search for truth has become a holy grail

Perhaps it is the nature of humanity
To always seek and never find clarity
Or maybe it is the universe's design
To keep us guessing and questioning all the time

A constant questioning, a never-ending fight,
To reconcile the chaos, the meaning, the why,
But the answers elude us, no matter how we try.

I see the world in shades of grey
Not black and white like some might say
There is no absolute truth, no divine plan
Just the chaos and complexity of human.

But is this nihilism, despair?
Or is it a chance to truly dare
To create our own meaning, our own path
To live in the moment, free from the aftermath.

I see this theme has been explored

The Socratic method, a search for truth
A journey to wisdom, through critical proof
But what if the truth is unknowable, unseen
An agnostic's mind, a constant seethe

Epicurus believed in pleasure and ease
But what if the world is just a disease
A temporary stop on our journey to death
Is living for pleasure, just one big test?

From Goethe's Faust, I ponder this question
Is there a divine plan, or just human obsession?
Mephisto speaks of a god that is dead
But Faust seeks the truth, and will not be misled
Faust grapples with the idea of faith
As he sells his soul to the devil, seeking power and knowledge
But in the end, he finds only despair and emptiness
Leaving him to ponder the ultimate cost of his college

And in Nietzsche's Thus Spoke Zarathustra
He speaks of the "death of God" and how it's a failure
For us to rely on a higher power, we must create our own meaning
And not succumb to the lies and false beliefs of others' demeaning
As he rejects the traditional values of morality
But his philosophy of the "Ubermensch" also falls short
Leaving us with nothing but chaos and futility

In characters like Camus' Meursault, so bold
He grapples with the meaning of it all
But finds no solace, no answers to call

Camus, and his Absurd Man
Who embraces the meaningless of it all
Life is a trap, he says, a Sisyphean task

But at least it's ours, to rise or to fall

Like Meursault, the stranger in Camus' tale
We live without purpose, without guilt or fail
We embrace the absurd, the meaningless void
But still we long for something, to be employed

The agnostic's doubt is often depicted, a constant struggle
In "The Outsider" by Camus, Meursault grapples
With the absurdity of life, no rhyme or reason to muddle

In "The Waste Land," Eliot asks, "Do I dare disturb the universe?"
For this is the ultimate curse.
Where the "dead tree gives no shelter" and "the thunder" is witty
A place where "the eyes that fix you in a formulated phrase"
Are "the eyes of a failed god," empty and void of grace
To believe in something greater, to have faith,
Is a decision that can be difficult to make.

Samuel Beckett, a writer revered
His words a source of contemplation
On the nature of existence and despair
And the struggle for salvation

In "Waiting for Godot," two men wait
For a savior they may never see
Their lives in a state of suspended fate
As they ponder what it means to be

"Endgame," a play of despair and loss
Characters trapped in a cycle of death
Their search for meaning, a constant toss
As they confront the final, chilling breath

Or consider Huxley's Brave New World,
Where truth is twisted and truth is twirled,
The characters live in a society that denies,
The existence of something beyond the sky.

In The Great Gatsby, Jay Gatsby's tale
A man who lived for love, but ultimately failed
In his quest for the impossible, he lost his way
A victim of his own, desperate desire to sway

But , I'm torn in two,
I want to believe, but what if it's not true?
I don't know the answers, and that's the rub,
It's a paradox that leaves me in a state of hub.

Or take Macbeth, a man of great ambition
Whose desire for power led to his demise
He thought to cheat fate, but in the end
His actions brought about his own demise

Or take Sartre's Roquentin, so lost and alone
In a world that seems meaningless, he is prone
To despair and hopelessness, but still he tries
To find some purpose, some reason to rise

And in Kafka's Metamorphosis, we see
The plight of a man turned into an insect
His life no longer holds meaning, it seems
As he struggles to find a way to reconnect

Like Hamlet, the prince of Denmark's despair
We question the meaning, the purpose, the care
Is life just a play, a fleeting performance
Or is there a grand design, a cosmic emergence

Like Holden Caulfield, the catcher in the rye
We search for the truth, but it eludes the eye
We reject the phony, the fake and the sham
But still we are left with the question, "Who am I?"

Macbeth, the tragic hero, wracked with guilt and shame,
Asks if life is but a walking shadow, a mere game.
Othello, the noble warrior, torn by jealousy and doubt,
Asks if it is worth the price of love, to shout.

In "Fathers and Sons," Bazarov grapples
With the weight of tradition and the freedom of new chapters
A nihilist, he denies all faith
But still struggles to find his own place

"What is the meaning of life? What is its goal?"
He asks, with a heart and mind full of soul
But the answers are never clear

Leaving him with doubts and fear

In "A Nest of Gentlefolk," Lavretsky
Is torn between love and duty
His heart aches for Pauline, yet he remains
Bound to his wife, a prison in her chains

I don't know what I believe
Marcel Proust writes of time, its fleeting and infinite
How it shapes and molds us, our choices and our limit

He writes of memory, how it's both a curse and a blessing
How it anchors us to the past, yet it's always guessing
What the future holds, what tomorrow may bring
It's a puzzle that we try to solve, but it's never a straight thing

We are all searching for something, a purpose, a meaning
But it's a journey that's never ending, it's never a clean thing
We struggle with doubt, with faith, with belief
We try to understand the world, but it's a never-ending thief

Celine's journey through the end of the night
Illuminates the struggles of this fight

He questions the meaning of it all
As he travels through the darkness of the world
The pain and suffering, the joy and delight
All seemingly meaningless in the end

But even as he grapples with these doubts
He finds moments of hope and connection
The love of a friend, the beauty of art
Glimmers of meaning in a chaotic world

Yet the questions still linger on
Is there a purpose or just random chance?
A God or just empty emptiness?
The paradox of life, a curse

In "Dead Souls," Chichikov wanders aimlessly
Searching for meaning, but finding only emptiness
His quest for wealth and status, a futile enterprise
Leaves him empty and alone, with nothing to show for it

In "The Overcoat," Akaky Akakievich's obsession
With material possessions, a false satisfaction
His pursuit of status, a meaningless obsession
Leaves him empty and alone, with nothing to show for it

Tolstoy's "War and Peace" to Dostoevsky's "The Brothers Karamazov"
The characters struggle, their faith in doubt
Searching for meaning, seeking a way out

Tolstoy's Prince Andrei finds no solace
In the grand ideals of war and peace
He seeks a higher purpose, a guiding light
But is left with only emptiness and fright

And Dostoevsky's Ivan grapples with faith
In a world that seems so filled with hate
He questions God, he questions his own soul
But can't find the answers, he feels alone

In "The Grand Inquisitor" by Dostoevsky
The agnostic's struggle is laid bare
The Grand Inquisitor declares faith a crutch, a lie
But the agnostic remains unsure, with no answer to spare

In "The Waste Land," Eliot writes of the "Unreal City"
A place where all seems lost and unsteady
Where the agnostic's faith is tested and tried
In a world where even the gods have died

But perhaps it is in the agnostic's doubt and questioning
That true meaning and purpose are found
For it is through the journey of self-exploration
That the agnostic's spirit becomes unbound

The Alchemist teaches us, to follow our hearts
To seek our Personal Legends, and not to depart
From the path that leads us, to our deepest desire
But is it truly worth it, to stoke the holy fire?

From the Ottoman, we see this struggle play out,
In the works of Rumi and Yunus, no doubts.
They grappled with the question, the conundrum of faith,
The mystery of existence, a riddle that escapes.

For Rumi, it was love that led him to the light,
A force that transcended reason, a divine delight.
He embraced the uncertainty, the mysteries of the soul,
Finding solace in the unknown, a goal.

Yunus, too, grappled with the paradox of life,
But in the end, it was submission that ended his strife.
He surrendered to the divine, accepting what he could not know,
Finding peace in the acceptance, a path to let go.

From the African , we see this theme
In characters like Okonkwo, of Things Fall Apart
He struggled with his doubts and beliefs
But ultimately, tradition won his heart

In The Wretched of the Earth, Fanon writes
Of the struggle for freedom and decolonization
But with this freedom comes a choice
To live in hope or despair, to find liberation

And in The River Between, Waiyaki grapples
With his Christian faith and traditional ways
He must find a balance, a harmony
Between the two, or else his soul will stray

From the Japanese , the tale of the fox
A creature of mystery, with nine tails, a paradox

It can be seen as wisdom, or trickery and deceit
But who can truly know, the truth is incomplete

The Tale of Genji, a tale of love and loss
The protagonist, a prince, at what cost
His search for happiness, a constant toil
But in the end, he finds only turmoil

The Haiku of Basho, a poem of brevity
Yet it holds so much, a philosophy
A moment captured, a fleeting moment
But in it, a lifetime of sentiments

The Zen of Dogen, a path to enlightenment
But is it truly attainable, or just a mere intention
The search for the self, a never-ending quest
But is the self even real, or just a test

From the Chinese literature, the Taoist sage
Teaches us to let go, to let life engage
To flow like water, to bend like a reed
To find balance and harmony, to fulfill our needs

But the Confucian scholar asks us to strive
To work hard and be virtuous, to be alive
To fulfill our duties, to honor our kin
To create order and harmony, to let goodness within

The struggles to find their own path

Between these two teachings, to escape life's wrath
To balance the yin and the yang, to let go and hold fast
To find the meaning of life, to make the journey last

the Bhagavad Gita
Explores this conundrum, as Arjuna contemplates
The nature of existence and his role in the world
Is it to fight, to kill, to conquer, or to be pearl

But Krishna counsels him, to do his duty
To fulfill his responsibilities, without seeking fruit or beauty
For in the end, it is not the outcome that matters
But the journey, the path, the choices we make and tatters

The Upanishads too delve into this mystery
Saying the self is not separate, but one with all history
That the ultimate goal is to realize this unity
To merge with the divine, to find serenity

I struggle to reconcile
These grand ideas with my own free will
Do I have agency, or is it all predetermined
These thoughts leave my head spinning, my soul imprisoned

In the Quran, it is written that "To Allah belongs the kingdom of the heavens and the earth. He creates what He wills. He bestows female (offspring) upon whom He wills, and bestows male (offspring) upon whom He wills" (42:49)

This verse speaks to the unpredictability of life
We cannot control who we are born to, or the circumstances of our birth
Yet, we are expected to live according to a certain set of rules and morals

Another paradox is found in the verse "And whoever kills a believer intentionally - his recompense is Hell, wherein he will abide eternally, and Allah has become angry with him and has cursed him and has prepared for him a great punishment" (4:93)

This verse speaks to the inherent value of human life
Yet, throughout history and even in present day, people continue to kill and harm one another
Why do we not value life as much as we should?

The Bible tells of life's great mystery
Of Adam and Eve, the first of humanity
Their sin brought forth the concept of mortality

But is it fair that we must all pay for their mistake?
Is it just that we must all suffer and die?
These questions plague me, they keep me awake

The Bible speaks of a God who is all-knowing and all-seeing
But how can we trust in a deity we cannot perceive?
Is it faith, or is it just believing
In something we cannot prove, but choose to believe?

The Bible tells us of a promised land
A place of eternal peace and joy
But how can we be sure this isn't just a grand
Fiction, a story meant to be enjoyed?

The Bible tells us of a savior who died for our sins
But is it really possible for one man to bear the weight
Of all the wrongs we've done, all the misdeeds and chins
That are scratched and scarred by the choices we make?

Or consider Job, in the Bible's pages
Whose faith is tested through countless ages
He questions the ways of the Lord on high
As he suffers, and wonders why, oh why

Buddhism teaches us of the Four Noble Truths
Of suffering, its cause, and how to find its roots
But as an agnostic, I struggle to believe
In a path to enlightenment, in a way to be free

I see the world, the beauty and the pain
But can't accept a single, ultimate gain
I'm torn between reason and faith, between doubt and trust
In a higher power, in a cosmic must

I seek answers, but they seem so far
I try to live in the present, but my mind's on the past or
The future, a never-ending cycle of confusion and fear
Is this all there is, or is there something more dear?

Sikhism offers solace, a path to follow
But my mind remains hollow
Of belief, a skeptic's creed
Unconvinced by holy deeds

Guru Nanak's teachings speak of truth
But do they hold any proof?
I cannot blindly accept
Without first using my intellect

The concept of karma, cause and effect
Is it true or just a suspect
I cannot know for certain
Without evidence, my faith is uncertain

The idea of reincarnation, a second chance
But how can we verify its stance?
Do we truly come back to life
Or is death the end, no more to strive

In Judaism, the Talmud speaks of free will
But how can we choose if God's plan is already sealed?
Is our destiny predetermined, or can we change our fate?
The paradox of life, it's hard to debate

The Kabbalah talks of balance and harmony
But how can there be balance in a world so harsh and mean?
Evil and suffering, they seem to prevail

The paradox of life, it's hard to unveil

The paradox of life is a difficult one to reconcile
For some, faith brings comfort and peace
But for me, it is a constant trial

I cannot blindly accept what is told to me
I must seek out the truth for myself
But in doing so, I may never be set free

From the endless cycle of questioning and doubt
But perhaps that is the beauty of life
We are all searching, never quite figuring it out

That life is a paradox, a mystery
A question mark, an enigma to see
We can search and seek, but we may never know
The answers to the questions that life doth throw

In uncertainty, a constant refrain
But perhaps the journey is worth the pain
For even in doubt, we can find our way
In the paradox of life, each new day.

So we live on, in uncertainty and doubt
But still we hope, and still we scout
The paradox of life, it may never be solved
But that doesn't mean our journey should be involved
For meaning, for purpose, for something more

In this paradox of life, an agnostic's lore.

44. Destined Love: A Universal Theme

In Japanese culture, the love of fate
Is seen in the concept of "shinju,"
Two hearts entwined as one,
Destined to be together, forever young.

In English, we speak of "destiny" and "kismet,"
The idea that love is meant to be,
No matter the distance or time,
Our hearts will always align, can't you see?

In French, "l'amour du destin" holds sway,
The belief that love is meant to be,
No matter the trials or the pain,
Together, forever, our hearts will stay.

In Indian culture, "karma" is key,
The belief that all actions have their reward,
And so it is with love, it is said,
That if it is meant to be, it will be restored.

No matter the language or culture we claim,
The love of fate is a universal theme,
A belief that with love, all things are possible,
And that together, our hearts will gleam.

45. Thomas the Train: A Journey Through Destiny

Thomas the train chugs along the tracks,
A small engine with a big heart,
He believes in freewill, the ability to choose,
To decide his own path, a new start.

But as he travels through the countryside,
He realizes that his choices are not his own,
The tracks dictate his course, his fate is predetermined,
His freewill is just an illusion shown.

He can't choose his destination,
He can't decide which route to take,
His every move is planned out,
His choices are for others to make.

Thomas wonders if he has control,
If he can truly be free,
But as he looks at the rails before him,
He sees that his fate is set, not up to he.

So he chugs along, accepting his role,
As the engine that follows the path laid before,
He may think he has freewill,
But in reality, he's just a pawn in a game of fate's score.

46. El Filosofía de la Fatalidad (The Philosophy of Fatality)

In mesoamerican, the love of fate
Is a recurring theme, one that relates
To the ancient belief that all things are ordained
By the gods, and that our lives are pre-explained

This belief is evident in many stories
Of the Aztecs and Maya, who found great glory
In the acceptance of their destiny and fate
Even if it meant sacrifice, war, or death's cold plate

For example, in the Aztec myth of Quetzalcoatl
The god was destined to leave and then return
To bring about the end of the world as we know it
But he accepted this fate and did not quit

Similarly, in the Maya myth of Hunahpu
The hero was destined to defeat the demon Vucub Caquix
And bring about the start of a new cycle of life
But he too accepted his fate and faced the strife

This love of fate can be seen as a philosophy
One that embraces the idea that everything is meant to be

That there is a reason and purpose for all that happens

And that we should not resist or try to change our path, but rather

accept and embrace it

But this philosophy can also be critiqued

For its potential to lead to fatalism and defeat

If we believe that everything is predetermined

Then what is the point of free will or making decisions?

Furthermore, this belief can be seen as oppressive

If it is used to justify injustice or to suggest

That those who suffer or are oppressed are doing so because it is their

fate

And thus, there is nothing that can be done to change their state

In conclusion, the love of fate in mesoamerican culture

Is a complex and multifaceted feature

One that can be seen as both a philosophy and a critique

Of the human condition and the role of fate in our lives, unique.

47. Embracing Destiny: A Love of Fate

Fate, a force that shapes our lives
A love that Nietzsche believed was right
For he saw it as the guiding light
That helps us reach our highest heights

But what is this love of fate, you may ask
Is it a love of destiny, or a love of the task?
For Nietzsche, it was both, a balance to be found
A love of the journey, not just the crown

He saw it as a way to overcome
The petty struggles of life, to become
Greater than we are, to rise above
The smallness of our fears, and show love

To the world, and all its wonders and its pains
To embrace the challenges, and not just the gains
For it is in facing adversity
That we truly grow, and reach clarity

So let us not shy away from fate's embrace
But rather, let us embrace it with grace
For it is through this love of fate
That we can truly elevate.

48. The Paradox of Life

The paradox of life, a conundrum that boggles the mind
To be or not to be, that is the question we find
Do we exist to simply exist, or do we have a purpose
Is life a journey or a destination, a game or a circus

Some say we are just atoms, colliding in the void
Others believe we are more, a soul that can be deployed
To fulfill a destiny, a calling that's divine
But is it truly free will, or just a predetermined line

Some say we are free agents, with choice and autonomy
Others say we are puppets, controlled by fate and destiny
But what is the true nature of life, and our role in it
Is it just a cosmic accident, or a grand design fit

Is life just a fleeting moment, a flash in the pan
Or is it something more, a journey that began
In the vast expanse of time, before we were born
And will continue long after, in the great beyond

The paradox of life, a riddle that may never be solved
But it's the journey that matters, the lessons that are involved
In the choices we make, and the paths we do choose
For in the end, it's not the destination, but the journey we lose

49. The Marionette Dilemma

Freewill, a concept held dear
A belief that we choose our path, that we steer
But is it true, or just a delusion?
A simple trick, a mere confusion?

Consider the metaphor of the puppet on a string
Moved by forces beyond our control, our movements not our own
thing
A puppet master pulling the strings
Determining our actions, dictating what the puppet brings

The idea of freewill, a grand illusion
Our choices predetermined, a predetermined conclusion
As the marionette moves to the puppet master's will
Freewill a mere figment, a concept still

This concept is not new, it's been debated for ages
From the pages of literature to modern day sages
In "The Brothers Karamazov," Dostoevsky asks
Is man a puppet, or more than a mere task?

And in "Hamlet," Shakespeare delves into the mind
As the prince ponders the weight of his own freewill defined
"To be or not to be," he contemplates with sorrow
The choices we make, do we truly borrow

So perhaps freewill is just an illusion
Our path predetermined, predetermined conclusion
But does it matter, in the grand scheme of things?
We can still make choices, and spread our wings

For even if our path is set, we still hold the power
To choose our actions, in any given hour
So let us embrace the concept of freewill
And make the most of it, until

The final curtain falls, and our time is through
Leaving a legacy, something we can do
Even if freewill is just an illusion
We can still make a difference, in our own version.

50. The Ship of Life's Odyssey

Like the ship of Perseus sailing on,
Life can be a journey long.
Full of ups and downs, twists and turns,
We must learn to weather all we face, and earn

The right to call ourselves true sailors,
Navigating the rough seas and the calmer waters.
For it is not the destination, but the journey,
That shapes us, teaches us, and helps us see

The world in a different light.
We must learn to weather the storms, and fight
To keep the ship afloat, no matter the cost.
For when we emerge from the dark and the frost,

We will have gained a strength and a wisdom,
That will serve us well in the days to come.
We will have learned the value of resilience,
And the importance of perseverance.

So let us embrace the ship of Perseus,
And all the lessons it has for us.
For it is through the struggles we endure,
That we become who we were meant to be, mature

And wise, ready to face whatever comes our way.

For life is a journey, and we must make the most of every day.

51. The Paradoxical Voyage of Identity

A paradox, a conundrum, a riddle to solve,
The Ship of Theseus, a tale to revolve.

The ship, once grand and true,
Now sits in a harbor, old and blue.

The question is asked, is it still the same?
For over time, its parts have changed, its hull and its frame.

The mast, the sail, the oars, the prow,
All replaced, but the ship, does it still somehow,
Retain its identity, its essence and soul?
Or is it a new vessel, no longer whole?

This puzzle, it seems, has no true end,
For whether the ship is the same, we cannot depend.

But perhaps, in the grand scheme of things,
It is not the ship that holds the identity it brings,
But rather the journey, the moments we share,
That shape and define us, beyond any repair.

So let us embrace the paradox, the mystery and the doubt,
And let the Ship of Theseus, forever sail about.

For in the end, it is not the vessel we see,

But the voyage, the lessons, and the legacy.

52. The Divine Duality: Lessons from Apollo and Dionysus

Two gods, so different, yet so wise,
Teach us lessons, before our eyes.
God Apollo, with his golden sun,
Brings us reason, second to none.

He teaches us to think and plan,
To be calm and measured, if we can.
To use our minds, to see the truth,
And to use our skills, to seek proof.

God Dionysus, with his vines and wine,
Brings us passion, a life divine.
He teaches us to live and love,
To let go and be free, like a dove.

To embrace our emotions, and let them flow,
To find joy and beauty, wherever we go.
To be wild and carefree, and to let our hearts sing,
To dance and celebrate, and to spread our wings.

Two gods, so different, yet so great,

Teach us lessons, that we can relate.
God Apollo, with his mind and light,
God Dionysus, with his heart and might.

Together, they show us the way,
To live a life full, each and every day.
To be balanced and whole, and to seek the best,
To learn from the gods, and pass the test.

53. The Quest for Truth: Navigating Agrippa's Trilemma

In ancient times, Agrippa posed a question,
A trilemma that still holds true today.
"Can we ever truly know the truth?" he asked,
"Or are our beliefs and understanding just a mask?"

This question is explored,
As characters seek answers and more.
In Shakespeare's Hamlet, the prince of Denmark
Wonders if he should believe in the ghost of his kin,

Or if it's just a figment of his imagination,
A product of his grief and frustration.
In Crime and Punishment, Raskolnikov debates
The morality of his actions, as he contemplates

Whether he can justify his deeds,
Or if they're just a product of his inner greed.
And in To Kill a Mockingbird, Atticus Finch
Encourages his children to seek the truth, to not flinch

From the challenges that come their way,
But to stand up for what they know to be true and just, each day.

Agrippa's trilemma is a timeless question,
One that we all must face, with every impression

We make, and every choice we choose,
Do we know the truth, or are we just confused?
It's a struggle that we all must face,
But it's one that can ultimately bring us grace,

If we seek the truth with an open heart and mind,
And leave behind the doubts and doubts we find.

54. The Timeless Truth

Beauty fades, it withers and it dies.
It's fleeting, ephemeral, and hard to define.
For some it's in the face, for others in the mind.
But true beauty lies within, where love and kindness reside.

For those who think they need to be fair and fine,
To be loved and admired, they are blinded by time.
For beauty is a state of mind, a way of being kind.
It's not about the way you look, but how you treat mankind.

So if you're ugly, do not despair,
For beauty is a fleeting thing, beyond compare.
It's something that we all possess, if we just dare.
To embrace it, nurture it, and let it flourish in the air.

So don't let others tell you what beauty is,
For it's something that's unique, and hard to miss.
Just be yourself, and let your light shine,
For true beauty is something that's always intertwined.

55. The Missing Piece: The Natasha Ryan Story and the Search for Existence

Natasha Ryan's case is one that's strange and unique
Her disappearance leaves a deep philosophical critique
What happened to her and where did she go?
These questions continue to haunt and grow

Her family and friends left to grieve and to mourn
As the years pass and her fate remains unknown
But in her absence, a story comes alive
Of the nature of existence and how we thrive

Some believe her spirit lives on, waiting to be found
Others see her case as a reminder of life's fragility and its bounds
Regardless of what happened, Natasha's story remains
A thought-provoking tale that will continue to remain

The strange case of Natasha Ryan will forever be etched
In the minds of those who consider what it means to be human, and how we connect
A philosophical epic that invites us to delve
Into the mysteries of life and our own personal hell

56. The Journey Within: A Guide to Self-Discovery and Worth

Life is a journey of discovery,
A path that's winding and unclear,
But one thing is certain, my dear,
You are worthy and loved, never fear.

Your imperfections, they make you unique,
Your scars and callouses, they tell your story,
You are stronger than you know,
And you are capable of achieving glory.

Don't let others define your worth,
You are deserving of happiness and love,
Take care of yourself, let your soul grow,
And search for what truly makes you thrive.

It's okay to ask for help,
And it's okay to take time to rest,
Be kind to yourself, and be your best,
You are loved, and that's the truth, I attest.

Life is a journey, and it's up to you,
To create the life that you desire,

Remember, you are worthy and loved,
Take the time to nurture your soul and inspire.

57. Embracing the Imperishable: The Power of Love and Memories

As I walk through this life, I realize
That material possessions don't matter, it's just a guise
We all strive for more, we accumulate stuff
But when we're gone, it's all gone, it's tough

What really matters is the love we shared
The memories we made, the bonds we bared
The way we made others feel, the way we shone
That's what lives on, that's what has grown

So let go of the things that weigh you down
Embrace the love, spread it around
For when we leave this world behind
It's not the stuff that we'll find

It's the love and memories that we leave behind
That will continue to thrive, to unwind
So let go of the material, embrace the love
For that is the only thing that will rise above.

58. The Ever-Evolving Journey: Embracing Change and Finding Purpose

But the world is never still, it's always changing
It's a constant battle to keep up and keep going
So I've learned to be strong, to stand tall
To keep moving forward, no matter how hard the journey may be

I've learned that sometimes, we must endure the pain
To find the beauty in the struggle, the growth in the strife
We must embrace the darkness, in order to see the light

For in the end, it's not about what we have or what we do
It's about who we are, and the mark we leave behind
So I choose to live my life with purpose and passion
To live, love, and learn, every single day

For it's in the journey, the highs and the lows
That we find ourselves, and discover our true selves
So let us embrace the unknown, and embrace the change
For it's in the unknown that we find our greatest growth.

59. Embracing the Journey: Lessons Learned

But as I sit here and ponder my past,
I realize that every challenge, every loss,
Has shaped me into the person I am today.
I've learned that life is not always fair,
But it's up to me to find the beauty in it.

I've learned that love is not always easy,
But it's worth the pain and heartache.
I've learned that sometimes we must let go,
To make room for new experiences and growth.

I've learned that it's okay to be vulnerable,
To let go of the facade and just be myself.
I've learned that it's okay to make mistakes,
As long as I learn from them and move forward.

So here I sit, ready to embrace the unknown,
Embracing the journey that is my life.
I know that there will be more ups and downs,
But I am ready to face them with open arms.
For I know that through it all, I am strong,
And I am capable of overcoming anything.

60. Embracing the Present: A New Dawn

But what is time, really?
A fleeting moment, a memory
A concept created by man
To measure the path of our journey

We can't hold onto it, try as we might
It keeps moving, no matter the fight
So why do we hold onto the past
Why do we let it hold us fast

It's time to let go, to move on
To embrace the present, a new dawn
Each moment is a gift, a chance to live
To love and be loved, to forgive

So let the past be, let it fade
Embrace the now, a new decade
Make the most of every moment, every day
Live and love in your own unique way.

61. The Beauty of Tranquility in a Turbulent World

Amidst the chaos and confusion,
In a world full of endless joys and woes,
There is a place of peace and solitude,
Where the mind can find its true voice.

It is the beauty of stillness,
A moment of calm in a stormy sea,
A respite from the constant chatter,
A place of clarity and tranquility.

In stillness, we find a sense of calm,
A sense of balance and perspective,
We can see the world with new eyes,
And find meaning in the smallest of things.

So let us seek out the stillness,
In the midst of all the noise,
For it is there that we can find,
Our truest selves and our innermost joys.

62. The Power of Inner Light

Your light, that shines within you
A beacon in the darkest of days
It guides you through life's challenges
And gives you hope in endless ways

But we must nurture and protect it
For the darkness will surely come
It will try to snuff out our flame
And make our spirit succumb

So hold on to your light dear one
For it is a precious gift
It will guide you through the shadows
And bring you back to the lift

Don't let the darkness consume you
For it will try to steal your shine
But if you keep your light burning bright
It will always be yours to find

So cherish your light, oh dear one
And never let it fade away
For it is a beacon of hope
That will guide you through each day.

63. Ode to the Playa del Amor

I yearn for the aesthetic splendor of Playa del Amor,
A secluded paradise the "Hidden Beach."
Nestled amidst the Marieta Islands of Mexico,
It is a sanctuary for the tranquility of the mind I seek to regain.

The cerulean waters and verdant landscapes,
A harmonious blend of natural beauty and serenity.
A haven for those seeking respite from the mundane,
A place where one can rediscover their inner serenity.

But alas, this idyllic paradise remains elusive,
A distant memory, a dream to be pursued.
But still I hold hope, that one day I will return,
To bask in the pulchritude of Playa del Amor anew.

For it is in this place of natural splendor,
That my soul finds solace and my mind peace to render.

64. Safe Haven in the Lake

In the depths of the lake,
A duck hides from the tiger's sake.
Deep below the surface so still,
The duck is safe and the tiger can't kill.

The duck swims with grace,
Leaving no trace.
The tiger roars and sniffs about,
But the duck remains hidden, no need to pout.

As the night wears on and the moon is high,
The duck knows it's time to fly.
It takes to the sky and soars away,
Leaving the tiger to hunt another day.

So the duck is free,
Safe and sound, you see.
It will hide in the lake again,
Until the tiger's threat comes to an end.

65. The Power of Love and Forgiveness

If someone strike you from the left cheek,
Give him the other also,
For it is not in anger that you speak,
But rather in a spirit of love and letting go.

For when we turn the other cheek,
We show that we are stronger than our fears,
That we will not be controlled by hate or meek,
But rather choose to rise above the tears.

For when we give our other cheek,
We open up a door of opportunity,
To show our attacker that we seek
To understand and love, not animosity.

So if someone strike you from the left cheek,
Do not let anger cloud your mind,
But rather offer up the other, meek,
And let love and kindness be your guide.

For in the end, it is not revenge that wins,
But rather the power of love and forgiveness,
Which will help us all to begin
A journey towards peace and happiness.

66. Love Thy Neighbor: A Call to Unity

Love your neighbor, as you love yourself
For this is the greatest command
It's not just about the words you say
But the actions you take, every day

Love your neighbor, with all your heart
For they are just like you, in every part
We are all brothers and sisters in this life
So let's strive to live without strife

Love your neighbor, as you love yourself
And together, we can build a world of wealth
Of love and compassion, and understanding too
A world where everyone's dreams can come true

So let's embrace this commandment with grace
And make this world a brighter place
Love your neighbor, as you love yourself
And watch the love in the world, multiply and excel.

67. Rising Above the Petty

A petty and sorry person,
Bite back when bitten,
Never able to rise above,
An animalistic love.

Insecurity and anger guide,
Their actions and their pride,
They cannot see beyond their nose,
And their ego grows and grows.

But the truly strong and wise,
Do not stoop to such lies,
They rise above the petty fights,
And choose to make things right.

So let the petty and sorry bite,
And let their malice ignite,
For they will only bring themselves down,
While the strong stand their ground.

For it takes a bigger heart,
To choose love and not take part,
In the childish games of bite and scratch,
And that is something to attach.

So let the petty and sorry fall,

Their actions speak for all,

While the strong and wise stand tall,

And rise above it all.

68. The Noiseless Journey: A Poem to the Patient Spider

O noiseless patient spider, spinning in the void
Trapped in a web of endless possibility
No destination, no end in sight
But still it spins, with all its might

For it knows that it is the journey, not the destination
That gives meaning to its existence
Every thread it spins and weaves
Is a step closer to its own belief

But what is belief, and what is truth?
Is it something we can see, or is it proof?
Perhaps it is something more abstract
Something that cannot be captured

So the spider spins, and spins and spins
Trapped in a web of its own design
But it does not despair, it does not grieve
For it knows that it is the journey that weaves

So let us be like the noiseless patient spider
Embrace the journey, let go of desire
For it is in the spinning, the weaving, the creating
That we find our true selves, and true meaning.

O noiseless patient spider, spinning in the void
A symbol of the journey, the journey we all employ.

69. Rising from the Crossroads: A Journey of Self-Discovery

I'm 29, and feeling lost
Midlife crisis, at what cost?
I've reached a crossroads, unsure of my path
Do I continue on, or turn back?

I look to the heroes of old
For guidance, for stories to be told
Of ancient philosophers, and the journey they took
To find their way, to find what they woke

Socrates, Plato, and Aristotle too
Their words of wisdom, still ring true
They searched for truth, and for meaning
And in the end, their legacy gleaming

But what of me, a mere mortal man
Trapped in this crisis, feeling out of hand
I seek the guidance of these greats
To find my way, and to relate

So I turn to their words, and their tales
And find solace in their wisdom, without fail

I take their lessons, and apply them to my life
And find the strength, to rise and fight

For this crisis, it is not the end
But a new beginning, a chance to mend
To find my path, and to follow through
To reach the top, and attain my true

So I embrace this crisis, and all it brings
I take control, and spread my wings
I rise to the challenge, and find my way
To the top, and to freedom, I'll find my way.

70. Soaring Beyond the Cycle

I'm just 29, and yet I feel
Like I've already reached the top of the hill
I've climbed and climbed, and yet I'm still
Trapped in this cycle, this never-ending thrill

I thought by now, I'd have it all figured out
But instead, I'm left with self-doubt
I thought success would bring me freedom
But instead, I feel like I'm suffocating, lost in a kingdom

I look around and see others thriving
But I feel stuck, like I'm not even surviving
What am I doing wrong, where did I go astray?
I thought I had it all figured out, but now I feel like I'm going astray

I turn to Marcus Aurelius for guidance and insight
His words offer solace, a beacon of light
"The universe is change; our life is what our thoughts make it."
This simple truth helps me see, I have the power to create it

I realize that I am the master of my own fate
I have the power to change, to create my own state
I don't need to reach the top to find freedom
It's within me, all along, I just need to find it and let it come

So I let go of my ego, my need to strive
I embrace the journey, let my soul thrive
I focus on the present, the now

And find peace in the journey, and the how

And with this newfound clarity, I find my way
I rise above, and start a new day
No longer trapped in this never-ending cycle
I am free, and I am whole, ready to soar and conquer life.

71. Rising Above: A Journey to Freedom

Mid-life crisis, oh how it gnaws
At the soul, at the very core
I'm 29, still so young
But already feeling like I'm done

Friedrich Nietzsche, he understood
The struggle, the search for something good
He wrote of the Übermensch, the superman
Who rises above, who takes a stand

But how do I reach the top, how do I fly
To that place of freedom, that place so high?
I'm trapped in this cycle, this daily grind
But Nietzsche teaches me to break free, to unwind

So I seek the path, the way to ascend
To reach the top, to find my end
I embrace my struggles, my doubts, my fears
For they are the stepping stones, the path to the clear

I am the master of my own fate
I create my own destiny, I seal my own fate
So I rise up, I break free
I am the Übermensch, I am free

And now for a creative and inspirational poem with an example from Friedrich Nietzsche:

I am the captain of my soul
I steer the ship, I reach my goal
I refuse to be held down
By doubts, by fears, by the ground

I am the Übermensch, the superman
I rise above, I take a stand
I embrace my struggles, my doubts, my fears
For they are the stepping stones, the path to the clear

72. Rising Above: Embracing Mid-Life Crisis for Growth and Freedom

Mid-life crisis, a time of doubt
A time to question all that we've learned
As we approach the age of 30
We start to wonder, where do we belong

But the Stoics say, don't fear the unknown
Embrace it, let it guide you on your way
For it is in the unknown that we find growth
And it is through growth that we find freedom

So let go of fear, and embrace change
It is the only way to reach the top
For it is at the top that we find true freedom
A freedom from the chains of society

So let go of your doubts, and rise to the challenge
Take control of your life, and don't let it manage
Use your mid-life crisis as a catalyst for growth
And you'll find that you'll reach the top, in no time at all

So don't let your age hold you back
Use it as a motivation to attack

The challenges that come your way
And you'll find that freedom is only a step away

Mid-life crisis, a time of opportunity
A time to embrace change and find unity
With ourselves and the world around us
So let go of your doubts, and rise above them

For it is in facing our fears that we find true freedom
And it is through freedom that we find true happiness
So embrace your mid-life crisis, and let it guide you
To the top, to a life of true freedom and joy.

73. Embracing the Unknown: A Journey to Freedom

Midlife crisis, oh how it plagues
The mind of a 29-year-old, trapped in a cage
Of self-doubt and uncertainty
Wondering if the journey's worth the agony

But as Albert Camus once said
"The only way to deal with fear is to face it head on"
So let us embrace this crisis with open arms
And find the strength to weather the storm

For it is in facing our fears and doubts
That we find the courage to rise above
To reach for the stars, and claim our freedom
To live our lives with purpose, and wisdom

So let us not be afraid of the unknown
But embrace it, and make it our own
For it is in taking risks and taking chances
That we find the path to true advancement

So let us rise up, and take control
Of our lives, and our destiny whole
For it is in reaching for the top
That we find true freedom, and never stop

74. The Rider's Journey: A Quest for Self-Discovery

A man of middle age
Trapped in a world that he couldn't engage
His dreams, they dwindled, his passions died
Leaving him lost, with no place to hide

But he could not give up, he could not resign
He knew there must be more, he knew he could shine
So he set out on a quest, a journey within
To find his true self, and to let his soul begin

He rode through the fields, he climbed every hill
He faced every challenge, he took every spill
He fought every demon, he conquered every fear
Determined to find the way, to make it clear

And as he rode, he began to see
That the journey was the key, to set him free
For it wasn't about the destination, but the ride
That helped him find himself, and let his spirit abide

So he rode on, through the highs and the lows
Through the triumphs and failures, he never let go
For he knew that the journey was the only way
To find his true self, and to live each day

So he rode on, until the end
And as he reached the top, he let his spirit ascend
For he had found the way, to attain true freedom
To live his life with purpose, and to let his spirit blossom.

75. Breaking Free: A Journey Through Midlife Crisis

Midlife crisis, oh how it plagues
The young and restless, trapped in cages
Yearning for freedom, for something more
But unsure of how to open the door

I am but 29, and yet I feel
Trapped in a life that is not real
The world around me spins so fast
Leaving me behind, a thing of the past

But I refuse to give in, to succumb
To this sense of stagnation, this feeling numb
I will find a way, I will reach the top
And in that moment, I will find my freedom, nonstop

I will shed the chains that bind me tight
And embrace the journey, with all my might
I will follow my heart, and let it lead
To the path of liberation, the path I need

So I will rise, and I will climb
To the top of the mountain, one step at a time
And when I reach the peak, I will stand tall
With freedom in my grasp, no chains to fall

For I am the master of my own fate
And in this journey, I will not hesitate
I will take control, and I will fly
To the top of the world, where the sky is nigh

So bring on the midlife crisis, bring on the pain
For I will face it all, and I will remain
Strong and determined, on my way to the top
Where freedom awaits, where my journey will stop.

76. The Writer's Journey: A 29-Year-Old's Midlife Crisis

A 29-year-old in midlife crisis
Feeling stuck, lost, and oh so vicious
Trapped in a world that doesn't understand
The struggles of a young man

But fear not, for there is a way
To reach the top, to find your way
To attain the freedom you desire
To set your soul on fire

Look to Fyodor Dostoyevski,
a man who knew the struggle
But found his way through the mire
To reach the top, to attain his freedom

He wrote and wrote, with all his might
Inspiring others to see the light
To find their own path, their own way
To reach the top, and make their day

So take heart, young man in crisis
For there is a way, there is a thesis
To find your way, to reach the top
To attain the freedom that you've sought

Just keep writing, keep creating
Inspiring others, keep motivating
For in the end, it is the journey
That sets your soul on fire, that makes you merry.

77. Rising from the Ashes: A Journey Through Midlife Crisis

Midlife crisis, oh how it grips
The heart and soul, a tumultuous trip
For a 29 year old, still young and bold
But feeling trapped, the future untold

Shakespeare knew this well, in his play "Hamlet"
The prince trapped in a world he can't stand it
"To be or not to be, that is the question"
A midlife crisis, a soul's depression

But we must push on, through the strife
For the journey to the top, is worth the life
For at the top, we find true freedom
A release from the chains, a new kingdom

So let us embrace the crisis, the turmoil within
For it is through this pain, we can begin
To see the world in a new light
And reach for the stars, with all our might

For midlife crisis is not the end
But a chance to start anew, to transcend

The limitations of our youth
And embrace the path, the journey, the truth

So let us embrace the crisis, the turmoil within
And rise up to the top, to attain true freedom.

78. The Journey Within: Embracing Midlife Crisis

Midlife crisis, oh how it lurks
A time of doubt, a time of fear
As I approach the age of thirty
I can't help but feel weighty

Marcel Proust said it best, "The real voyage of discovery
Consists not in seeking new landscapes,
But in having new eyes."
But how do I find these new eyes,
To see the world with fresh delight?

I've spent my youth chasing success
But now I find myself in a mess
Trapped in a life that's not my own
Yearning for something more, something shown

But where do I start, how do I find
The path that leads to peace of mind?
I've tried to climb the ladder of success
But all I find is endless stress

So perhaps it's time to let go
Of all the expectations, the societal flow
To find my own way, to follow my heart

To finally find the freedom I've been seeking from the start

For it's not about reaching the top
But about finding a path that never stops
A path of self-discovery and growth
A path that leads to inner peace, to a life well-known

So I'll embrace this midlife crisis
As a chance to start anew
To find my own path, my own truth
To finally find the freedom I've been seeking, my own proof

For it's not about reaching the top
But about finding a path that never stops

79. Bald and Bereft: A Lament for Bygone Locks

Alas, the bald man ponders o'er his past,
With naught but memories of hair full-grown,
A lavish mane that danced in winds aghast,
A crown of splendor, now forever flown.
But still, he clutches to the strands he's cast,
And weaves a tapestry of days unknown.

In solitude, he gazes at his pate,
And strains to recall each golden strand,
Each lock that swayed with every step he'd take,
And held the secrets of his soul so grand.
He longs to touch the hair that once was great,
And finds solace in the memories at hand.

The man once reveled in his silken tress,
And with each strand, he wore his pride so bold.
But now, he's left with nothing to possess,
And stares at emptiness, so bare and cold.
He thinks of days that passed, of happiness,
And wonders how his hair could be so old.

He remembers how he'd bask in summer rays,
And bask in sun-kissed hues of chestnut brown.
His hair, a symbol of his youthful ways,

A beacon of his life, now lost and found.
But now, the man is left with naught but grays,
And traces of a life, now tattered and bound.

He wonders if his hair had been a curse,
A fleeting gift that time had taken back.
Or if it was a gift, so fair and scarce,
A treasure that he could not bring back.
And as he ponders, he begins to traverse,
The labyrinth of thoughts that leave him slack.

He thinks of all the things he could have done,
With hair as lush as summer fields in bloom.
Of all the roads he could have just begun,
And all the dreams he could have met with room.
And as he thinks, his heart begins to swoon,
And he is lost, in memories that loom.

The bald man clutches at his balding head,
And thinks of all the strands that he has shed.
He thinks of all the things that might have led,
To this, a life bereft of hair and bed.
And as he thinks, he's filled with thoughts of dread,
And wonders if he'll ever find his way.

Thus, the bald man stays, in memories caught,
Of hair so full, so vibrant, and so rare.
And though his hair is gone, his mind is fraught,
With memories of days, so bright and fair.

And though he'll never have his hair again,
The memories will always be his treasure.

The bald man weaves a tale, of strands and sheen,
A story of his hair, so rich and bright.
A chronicle of days, so full and green,
A life, now lost, in shadows of night.
And as he tells his tale, so soft and keen,
He finds solace in the memories of light.

He thinks of all the moments, sharp and clear,
Of all the laughter, and the joys untold.
He thinks of all the love, so pure and dear,
And all the dreams, now buried, grown so cold.
And as he thinks, he wipes away a tear,
For all the hair, that's now forever old.

The bald man ponders, as he sits alone,
And thinks of all the days, that have passed by.
He thinks of all the hair, that once had grown,
And all the dreams, that once could touch the sky.
And as he thinks, he finds a seed that's sown,
A seed of hope, that still can make him fly.

So, the bald man rises, with a smile so bright,
And walks towards the future, with his head held high.
For he knows, that though his hair is gone,
His memories will always be with him, and nigh.
And though he'll never have his hair again,

His memories will always be his treasure.

Thus, the bald man continues on his quest,
With memories of hair, that once was blessed.
A life, now lost, but still, the best,
A journey, rich with tales, that still possess.
And as he travels, he'll always possess,
The memories of hair, that once was yester.

The bald man finds solace, in the tales he's spun,
A tapestry of memories, so dear and true.
For though his hair may be gone, he has begun,
To cherish all the moments, that once he knew.
And as he walks, he feels his spirit won,
By all the memories, that still come through.

He thinks of all the times, that made him smile,
And all the laughter, that once filled his soul.
He thinks of all the love, that stayed awhile,
And all the dreams, that made him feel so whole.
And as he thinks, he feels his heart beguile,
By all the memories, that still make him whole.

So, the bald man journeys, with a heart so light,
And walks towards the future, with his head held high.
For he knows, that though his hair is gone,
His memories will always be with him, and nigh.
And though he'll never have his hair again,
His memories will always be his treasure.

Thus, the bald man walks, with tales untold,
Of hair so full, and memories so bright.
A life, now lost, but still so bold,
A journey, rich with tales, that still ignite.
And as he walks, he'll always hold,
The memories of hair, that once was bright.

And so, the bald man continues on his way,
With memories of hair, that still live on.
A life, now lost, but still so gay,
A journey, rich with tales, that still are strong.
And though his hair may be gone astray,
His memories will always be his song.

80. Mysteries of Pica: An Enigma Unveiled

In the realm of medical curiosities,

Pica stands tall as a mysterious enigma,

A condition that brings with it both worries

And fascinations, arising from the embolism

Of the human psyche, where hunger often lies.

A condition of consuming inedible items,

It leaves many to ponder and theorize

On its origins, seeking to unravel its cryptogram

For the sake of the children it affects.

Some say it stems from mineral deficiencies,

Others attribute it to a lack of emotional warmth,

But still, there remains much left to theorize

As to why such strange cravings persist and amplify

In the minds of those who suffer from pica's psychogram.

For children, it can lead to serious health hazards

As they consume items such as paper, glue, or chalk,

Making it imperative to find a cure or therapy.

Science has attempted to explain pica's complexities

By delving into the brain and its neural pathways,

Uncovering a possible connection to obsessive compulsive disorders,

But the truth remains shrouded in mystery and ambiguity.

From a philosophical perspective, it raises questions

On the nature of human desire, and how it often defies
Logic and reason, leading us down unpredictable ways.

One might ask, why do we crave what we cannot eat?
Why do we yearn for that which brings us no sustenance?
Is it a manifestation of some deeper, unconscious need?
Or simply a result of societal and environmental factors that unbalance
Our physiological and psychological systems?
The answers, much like the condition itself, lie cryptic.

But we must not forget the plight of the children affected,
For whom pica brings only suffering and fear.
We must strive to understand its complexities,
And seek to find a cure, a way to alleviate their distress.
For it is not just a medical condition, but a social and ethical issue
That demands our attention, and a philosophical and scientific
resolution.

Thus, as we delve deeper into the cryptic realm of pica,
We must remember the children who suffer in its grasp,
And strive to unravel its mysteries, to bring them relief and hope,
For a brighter future, free from the pains of this condition.
For in our quest to understand the complexities of pica,
We may discover not only its cure, but a deeper truth about the human
psyche.

As we delve deeper into the cryptic realm of pica,
We must consider the various theories and hypotheses
That attempt to explain its origins and complexities.

Some posit that it is a result of cultural and societal conditioning,
Others point towards psychological and emotional disturbances.
But the truth remains elusive, shrouded in mystery and ambiguity.

From a scientific standpoint, it is fascinating to theorize
On the possible neural pathways and brain functions
That contribute to the manifestation of this condition.
Is it a result of genetic predisposition or environmental influences?
Is it a manifestation of some deeper, unconscious need?
The answers to these questions lie cryptic,
Leaving us with much to uncover and unravel.

But as we ponder the scientific and philosophical implications of pica,
We must not forget the impact it has on the affected children.
For they suffer greatly, consumed by a condition they cannot control,
Bringing harm to their bodies and causing emotional distress.
It is imperative that we strive to find a cure,
A way to alleviate their suffering and bring them hope.

One potential avenue for exploration is the role of nutrition and diet,
As many have suggested that pica may stem from mineral deficiencies.
Is it possible that replenishing the body with the proper nutrients
Could help to mitigate the symptoms and cravings of pica?
It is a possibility worth considering, as it offers a tangible solution.

Another avenue of inquiry lies in the realm of psychology and therapy,
For it has been suggested that pica may be a manifestation of deeper
emotional wounds.
Is it possible that addressing and healing these wounds

Could help to alleviate the condition and bring peace to the affected children?

It is a possibility that merits investigation and exploration.

The realm of pica is one of great philosophical and scientific interest,

As it raises questions on the nature of human desire and the human psyche.

But our inquiry must not neglect the impact it has on the affected children,

For whom pica brings only suffering and fear.

We must strive to understand its complexities, and seek to find a cure,

For a brighter future, free from the pains of this condition.

Thus, we must approach pica with a balance of scientific and philosophical inquiry,

For only through a combination of both can we hope to unravel its mysteries

And bring relief to the children it affects.

For the truth about pica lies cryptic, but with our combined efforts

We may one day unlock its secrets and bring hope to those in need.

In our quest to unravel the mysteries of pica,

We must consider the cultural and societal implications of the condition,

For it may shed light on the underlying psychological factors that contribute to its manifestation.

Is it possible that societal norms and cultural values play a role in the development of pica?

Or does the condition stem from a deeper, universal human

experience?

The answers to these questions lie cryptic, waiting to be discovered.

Moreover, we must examine the role of trauma and abuse in the development of pica,

For it has been suggested that such experiences may contribute to the manifestation of the condition.

Is it possible that pica serves as a coping mechanism for individuals who have suffered traumatic events?

Or is it simply a manifestation of deeper, unconscious emotional disturbances?

The answers to these questions lie cryptic, shrouded in mystery and ambiguity.

Additionally, the role of societal attitudes and stigmas towards mental health must not be overlooked,

For they may play a significant role in the manifestation of pica.

Is it possible that societal attitudes towards mental health contribute to the development of pica by discouraging individuals from seeking help?

Or do societal attitudes have no impact on the manifestation of the condition?

The answers to these questions lie cryptic, and require further investigation.

As we continue our quest to understand the complexities of pica,

We must also consider the impact it has on the affected individuals and their families,

For they suffer greatly, and often in silence, due to societal stigmas and discrimination.

Is it possible that providing support and resources for those affected by pica

Could help to mitigate the symptoms and cravings of the condition, and bring hope and relief to the affected individuals and their families? It is a possibility that requires attention and exploration.

Thus, as we delve deeper into the cryptic realm of pica,
We must approach it with a combination of scientific and philosophical inquiry,
And consider the cultural, societal, and psychological implications of the condition.
For only through a holistic approach can we hope to unravel its mysteries
And bring relief and hope to the affected individuals and their families.

In conclusion, pica remains a mysterious and enigmatic condition,
With much left to be uncovered and understood.
But as we continue our quest to understand its complexities,
We must keep in mind the impact it has on the affected individuals and their families,
And strive to find a cure, a way to alleviate their suffering and bring them hope.
For the truth about pica lies cryptic, but with our combined efforts,
We may one day unlock its secrets and bring relief to those in need.

Khublei Shihajar Nguh

Thank you, dear reader, for taking the time
To journey with me through these lines.
Your attention and patience, I do implore,
For it's your support that I adore.
You've completed reading this book with care,
And I'm grateful that you were there.
To experience these reflections, so true,
Of the complexities of the human hue.
So I ask, as you close these pages with glee,
Do read other books in this series, you'll see.
The journey continues, with much to impart,
Of the human experience and the human heart.
And don't forget, dear reader, to explore
Other books by this author, even more.
For each one brings a different light,
To shed on the world, day or night.
So thank you again, dear reader, I say,
For taking this journey with me today.
May your life be filled with much to discover,
And may these words bring you solace and wonder

Note

As I, a breviloquent raptor, wield A lever, with naught else to my design, I generate tones for the aural field In this prosaic orb we call mankind. My actions, though, are but a small part Of forces far beyond my control, For nature holds the key to each chart And sets the laws that govern the whole. But still, I am compelled to explore The workings of this vast machinery, To seek the truth that lies at core And find the answers to humanity. Though some may call it quest I'll seek the truth, with no time to rest.

About The Author

Meet Mawphniang Napoleon, a man of many talents and passions. As a lawyer and entrepreneur, he has achieved success in the professional world, but his true passion lies in writing and humanism. He is a soul ever-striving, never at ease, with boundless curiosity and verve. He embraces new ideas with an open mind and ventures boldly into unknown lands. He is passionate about seeking all that life has to offer, cherishing the small things and on a journey of self-discovery. He writes his story with fearlessness and making the most of every moment, ever-unfurled. He is originally from Syadheh village, Ri Bhoi District in Meghalaya, India.

P.C : Clarissa Candace Giri

www.ingramcontent.com/pod-product-compliance
Lightning Source LLC
Chambersburg PA
CBHW051154130726
47988CB00005B/2125